Me

THE ART OF LIVING SERIES
Series Editor: Mark Vernon

From Plato to Bertrand Russell philosophers have engaged wide audiences on matters of life and death. *The Art of Living* series aims to open up philosophy's riches to a wider public once again. Taking its lead from the concerns of the ancient Greek philosophers, the series asks the question "How should we live?". Authors draw on their own personal reflections to write philosophy that seeks to enrich, stimulate and challenge the reader's thoughts about their own life.

Published
Clothes   *John Harvey*
Death   *Todd May*
Deception   *Ziyad Marar*
Fame   *Mark Rowlands*
Hunger   *Raymond Tallis*
Illness   *Havi Carel*
Me   *Mel Thompson*
Middle Age   *Christopher Hamilton*
Pets   *Erica Fudge*
Sport   *Colin McGinn*
Wellbeing   *Mark Vernon*
Work   *Lars Svendsen*

Forthcoming
Faith   *Theo Hobson*
Money   *Eric Lonergan*
Sex   *Seiriol Morgan*
Science   *Steve Fuller*

Me

Mel Thompson

ACUMEN

First published in 2009 by Acumen

Acumen Publishing Limited
Stocksfield Hall
Stocksfield
NE43 7TN
www.acumenpublishing.co.uk

ISBN: 978-1-84465-166-5

British Library Cataloguing-in-Publication Data
A catalogue record for this book is available
from the British Library.

Typeset in Warnock Pro.
Printed in the UK by the MPG Books Group.

Contents

Acknowledgements

I am grateful to David Llewellyn-Jones, whose probing questions helped shape an early draft of this book, to Mark Vernon for his encouragement and insightful suggestions, and to Steven Gerrard at Acumen for bringing it to publication.

Mel Thompson

Introduction

I am fascinated by photography: the attempt to capture a fleeting reality, to freeze action, but most of all to record the experience of a moment that is already drifting towards the vortex of the past. Photographs of people are the most challenging and frustrating. In a good photographic portrait there is the sense that the look, the gesture and the setting all reveal a "real" person. "Yes, you've captured him exactly", I say, as I look at the image of someone I know well. Like a painting, a photograph can convey more than the pixels that make it up. I scan the image for clues to the reality of the person who is now reduced to two dimensions, fixed and mute.

A recent exhibition of photographs from Eastern Europe before the Second World War included images of peasants in rough clothes, faces weathered, hands calloused, thoughtful, suspicious of the camera being pointed their way, proud, solid but also wary, vulnerable. Alongside them, other photographic images were clearly contrived, working with abstract shapes or photomontage. All were making a political point, but it was the peasant images that spoke most eloquently of life in that place and time. Whether taking photographs or looking at them, I make the assumption that each person has some unique essence, a character that may be revealed in – but not entirely defined by – the physical circumstances and appearance that the camera records. But what is it that enables an image to show a "real character"? It is difficult to define, yet instantly recognizable.

I go through that same process whenever I encounter someone I know, for the instant of recognition brings with it the remembrance of a shared history, moments of personal disclosure or deception, acts of kindness or cruelty. A relationship is built on shared experiences that memory provides for me as soon as I approach that person in the present. The face is everything; the moment of recognition changes my whole response to an approaching figure. I immediately know that I am encountering a "person" and they are encountering "me".

And yet, as I look at a photograph or encounter someone face to face over a coffee, I am always open to being surprised. There may be an aspect of that person that I have not seen before, depths that I have not explored. And equally, there is so much that I carry with "me" that I have yet to share with them. We can never fully know or be known. And that's the puzzle and frustration. I can recall shared moments, guess what my friend is likely to say on any given topic and feel the emotional warmth of mutual acceptance, but I am also aware that I can choose to hide aspects of myself, and that my friend can do the same. Even un-retouched photographs or film can lie. One year, in my early teens, I wanted a tape recorder for Christmas. I dropped hints and debated with my father the merits of a tape recorder over a record player. He claimed the latter to be far more useful; I belonged to a choir and wanted to record live performances. Christmas came, and the old home movie shows me smiling to camera as I unwrap the record player. My anger and frustration remain completely hidden. My inner experience of that moment is quite unlike the obvious interpretation of the scene depicted on film. I was not what you see. And if then, what of now? And if me, what of you?

To be genuine, rather than to deceive; to be open rather than closed; to be cautious about revealing one's feelings or to do so recklessly in love: all these experiences assume that there is a knowable person – that the "you" I encounter, and the "me" that you encounter are genuinely knowable entities. But I am forced to recognize the gap between what I am and what others perceive, and therefore I am forced to acknowledge the gap between what I perceive of others and what they are in themselves.

The more we reflect on the nature of the self, the stranger it becomes. There have been many different approaches to understanding personal identity. The dualist approach emphasizes the difference between the thinking mind, self or soul on the one hand and the physical body on the other. Caricatured by Gilbert Ryle in *The Concept of Mind* (1949) as the doctrine of the "ghost in the machine", it struggles with the problem of how we know other persons and what the self might be like if separated from its physical body. At the other extreme, a materialist approach argues that the self is no more than a convenient label to stick on a portion of physical reality, and that, with the aid of developments in neuroscience, all the wonders of the human mind and spirit will eventually be revealed as patterns of activity within the brain. But can either approach do justice to the self that we experience, and the selves that we encounter around us?

To consider the nature of the self, it is therefore not enough to argue about how mind relates to matter, or whether it would be possible for the same self to inhabit different bodies, or whether we are free or determined, or whether neuroscience can fully explain consciousness. These have been stock issues in the philosophy of mind, and they are perfectly valid questions to ask, but they do not seem to me to engage immediately with the more personal, existential questions: how do I make sense of my life; am I responsible for the person I have become?

In a world where randomness and chance make life transient and unpredictable, religion, psychology and philosophy have all tried, in their different ways, to give meaning and coherence to the human person. The question is not just "Who am I?" but also "What is my life for?" and "What is worth doing?" When I set myself goals or make decisions, I need to believe that I am shaping my future, otherwise I see myself as no more than a puppet, jerking in response to the strings of circumstance. Whether or not there is a puppeteer, of course, be it God or fate, is another matter. To me, the art of living and the goal of every personal philosophy is to construct a meaningful "me": to make sense of my life. How that may be done is the question that this book addresses. But let us go back one step and examine the process by which the experiencing self constructs its "me".

There is a small bunch of lily of the valley on the table in front of me as I write: delicate creamy-white flowers, illuminated by horizontal shafts of early spring sunshine, the light shaping each bell. And as I look at them I am aware that they give me pleasure. But almost immediately I am reminded of myself aged perhaps three or four, walking in the woods near my childhood home, holding my grandmother's hand, and looking down on the delicate woodland carpet of white and green lily of the valley. So the flowers evoke positive memories of childhood and I start to feel comfortable in myself; I am still here almost sixty years later, the same person that saw them as a child. They are part of what it is to be me.

I notice that the tiny flowers sit in a liqueur glass, and think (at this early hour!) of having a drink, of buying liqueur as a student on a camping holiday, of sipping green chartreuse and thinking then of monasteries, and monks engaged in silent work producing the delicate liquid, gathering the herbs. And I remember again the attractions of the monastic life – silence, and stone steps, and the quiet pace of robed figures beneath a gothic arch, and the fantasy of a disciplined, purposeful life – sensed in my youth as a possible vocation, but later abandoned. And then I think of the many other things that have been lost or set aside as the years have passed, and of my own hectic lifestyle: the choices, good or bad, that have shaped my life, that have defined my path. Impressions, memories and longings come flooding in at the sight of these particular flowers.

Association and memory locate each experience within a personal web of meaning, and when they cannot do so we feel lost and alienated. New experience is fleeting. Almost as soon as we have it, it is colonized by our memory and we start to incorporate it into a personal map that we are constantly revising, which depicts our terrain of meaning and significance. It is given a place within a very personal set of grid references, relating it to who we are. This is the process that links experience to memory and identity, giving each of us a unique sense of self.

I am a being that watches and moves, that seeks out what it needs, that makes its home, that raises its offspring, that has hopes and fears, aims and goals. But there is a real problem here. As I experience it, the public self that I construct would seem to be the product of the personal decisions that I make. But is that really the case, or is it a delusion, masking an objective, scientifically predictable self?

Psychologists, sociologists, politicians and, particularly, marketing executives know precisely who I am and who I will be as I get older. I am predictable. I am one of a category of people who is likely to prefer product A to product B, and who is likely to be watching television at a particular time and therefore to be exactly on target for that product placement. I am analysed within national statistics. The changes that I experience in myself are explicable: some through biology, as I grow older, others through social pressure. It was absolutely predictable that I should have had long hair and a beard at one time, not through personal choice, but because I was a student in the 1960s, when such things, along with my purple flared trousers, were a social obligation. At the time, I experienced them as my freely chosen rebellion against the style of the previous generation, but with hindsight I was simply obeying the command of a social trend. So am I free to choose and shape myself, or is it all determined and predictable?

If I apply for a job I may be required to produce a curriculum vitae, an account of what I have done with my life thus far, on the assumption that it will show whether I am going to be a suitable person, appropriately qualified for the post that is available. It should be an honest and objective account of my career. But that's not all the interviewers are going to want to know. They're also after the personal angle. How do I come across? Am I "open" to them? Is the personal chemistry going to be right when I mingle with others on the staff? Am I the person they're looking for? So what do they do? They set psychometric tests, role plays and simulation exercises. They send me off to have coffee, innocently giving me a break from the interview process, only to monitor me once away from the tension and need to perform. "How was he socially?", they'll ask afterwards. And in all this they are desperately looking for "me", as much as I am scanning that photograph for some hint at the real person who stares up at me from the print. So the objective curriculum vitae is not in itself sufficient in assessing whether I am suitable for the job. They want the personal: the intuitive sense of "me". But even if they get that right, am I going to remain the person they now believe me to be?

People seem to want a definite and fixed idea of who I am. Yet all I know, from science and from observing the world around me, is that my life is by no means fixed; it is in a continual state of flux. So here is the dilemma. To shape and direct my life I need a concept of "me" (and so does my potential employer). Without that, I cannot know what to do, what to choose. And yet, I also know that nature and time will rob me of that fixed idea. I am not in control of my life. At every moment things impact on me that can change everything: a disease, an accident, a financial crash, a lapse of concentration while driving, an earthquake. At every moment we are vulnerable and changing. We are never exactly what we thought we would become. Life now is never what we once assumed life in the future would be. The world moves on and changes our lives in the process.

But can I let go of the need for "me"? Is it possible to live in the present moment, sensitive only to the world that is to hand, flowing with it in complete unselfconsciousness? Such a view is in line with Taoist or Buddhist philosophy, where liberation comes from recognizing that, in a world of constant change, there can be no fixed self.

Memory and hope alternately shape our experience. We are as we are now because of our past; but what we choose to do now reflects what we hope to be in the future. Neither past nor future exist in the present moment, yet both influence what I am now. So what is it to be "me"? How does it relate to the ever-changing sequence of experience and emotion that I have? "He's getting to be a real little person", they say of my step-grandson of six months, and I know what they mean. He sits up now, takes notice, spots people across the room and smiles, watching with apparent interest the activities of the adults around him. But how has that development from a tiny baby aware only of his own needs and sensations to an individual that relates to the outside world come about? And will that process continue throughout his life? Am I still becoming a real, not-so-little person? And, if so, can I shape that process? These are the questions we need to address.

1. Getting beyond our neurons

The conversation around the table seems distant now. From time to time I make an effort to listen to what is being said, but it does not last. A feeling of dullness settles on me; I'm becoming bored. My eyes remain open, my ears still hear the conversation, but now I start thinking of what I will do tomorrow. I consider various options, silently talking to myself; the monologue seemingly going on within my head. Without entirely losing my present experience (I have not actually fallen asleep) my mind superimposes other scenes over that of the assembled company at the table. I am remembering, planning, enjoying a fantasy that is more real and vivid to me than my present experience. But suddenly I am aware of someone leaning across and asking me a question. "I'm sorry," I say, unable to hide my inattention, "I was miles away".

But where was I? Clearly, I was still in the same physical position; my body had not shifted, but my mind had loosened its connection with the ongoing stream of present experience and was ranging over a terrain of its own, visualizing people and places, some already known to me, some imagined. In my mind I was elsewhere. I know I am this physical body – that's not in doubt; and I have not left the table. Asked where I am, others could point to me without hesitation. This body is what they identify as "me" (along with all its habits, including daydreaming). But is my body really "me", or am I something quite different, merely hiding within this physical shell?

Let's start our enquiry by stating the obvious. I am a physical being. Bounded by my skin, I am a complex biological organism, a constantly changing and developing set of systems that maintain me as a living thing. My blood circulates, my lymph drains, my digestive system processes food and provides nutrients to keep me going. Like all living things, I exist by receiving nourishment from the outside world. My life expectancy, once deprived of oxygen, is a few minutes at most. Whirring away within my head is that miracle of organic complexity, a human brain. It consumes a substantial part of my energy, and controls my physical systems. Without the constant contact that it has with the rest of my body I am dead, as the guillotine or noose effectively illustrate. We know that we are physical bodies, but are we more than that? Is there something about being "me" that goes beyond what can be analysed in terms of the functioning of my brain and the rest of my body? The view that we are nothing more than the body is termed materialism.

Daniel Dennett argued in *Consciousness Explained* (1991) that the mind is the brain and that there is only one sort of stuff, namely physical matter. What we experience when we experience ourselves is simply matter, whirring into life as neurons connect with one another. There is no ghostly or private "self" or "mind": that is an illusion generated by the sheer complexity of the brain, and one day a perfect neuroscience will tell us all that we need to know about ourselves. Indeed, in *Freedom Evolves* (2003), he caricatures the idea of souls, calling them "spectral puppeteers", externally manipulating physical bodies.

In the most extreme form of this approach, called "eliminative materialism", mental phenomena, including our thoughts, feelings, intentions, hopes and so on, do not exist: they are simply ways of describing neural activity. And if neurobiology could show exactly how each part of the brain controlled feelings, thoughts and so on, there would be no need for any further explanation of what we call mind. Essentially, we are the trillions of mindless robots toiling away in our brains, and nothing else. Materialism tends towards scientism: the claim that the use of the scientific method is the only way of understanding our world. By contrast, this book will argue that science – however valid in its own terms – is not the most useful tool for understanding "me".

Some thinkers demonstrate their views in unusual ways. In the Abbie Museum of Anatomy at the University of Adelaide, there is a curiously philosophical exhibit: a brain. It is not philosophical in itself, of course, but the caption below it reads, "Did this Brain Contain the Consciousness of U. T. Place?" Place, a professor of that university who took a particular interest in the philosophy of mind and who died in 2000, argued for a materialist view. Perhaps, in a science-fiction future, his brain may be hooked up to an equally sophisticated but living computer, and Place will be reconstructed. My guess is that all that could ever be found behind that glass is an elaborate computer, without an operating system or software: impressive but quite unable to run.

I am a physical body, but one that is related to the rest of the world through my senses. My sense of touch is located all over my skin, particularly in my hands, but the other senses – sight, smell, taste and hearing – are located around my head. I tend to think of myself as inhabiting my head. It is from my head that I get my sense of direction, locate myself within the world and move around. The head, and particularly the face, is also the means by which I communicate with others. Every tiny facial gesture expresses something that I am thinking. There is no scope here to dwell on how absolutely amazing the head is (to appreciate that, there is no better book than *The Kingdom of Infinite Space* by Raymond Tallis). So should I define "me" simply in terms of what happens inside my head?

Thoughts and feelings relate to more than neural activity: tears may be produced, muscles may cause people to tremble with fear, sweat may break out, sexual organs may prepare themselves for an anticipated opportunity of action. Perhaps all of these things may happen at once! The emotional life of a human being involves the whole body. The brain may control our life, but does that imply that we are "nothing but" brain activity? I have a dilemma, and therefore worry about what to do; my body reflects the resulting anxiety. But is that dilemma *initiated* by brain activity? Of course not. The brain responds to external circumstances, conveyed to it through the senses. It reacts to the situation that "I" find myself in as I engage with the world. "I" am the one that gives my brain the dilemma. Even if "I" cannot be pinpointed in space and time – that is, even if I can find no separate place for "me" within my skull that is not already occupied by brain matter doing its work – it is still the fact that I am in the world, relating to others, that gives the processing engine of the brain something to chew on. That "me" is myself in my world.

Exploring the way in which the brain responds to these stimuli, analysing its operation rather on the computer model, is termed "functionalism" and is an approach taken by Hilary Putnam and others. The brain receives signals from the sense organs, processes them and initiates appropriate responses. I put my hand too near the fire: my brain receives messages to the effect that nerve endings in the hand are being damaged, and it responds by contracting my arm muscles to remove my hand from the flame. Functionalism therefore gives a way of mapping out what the brain does. We cannot "see" thought in the firing of neurons; all we can measure is the pattern of stimulus and response that is going on. Taken beyond the simplicity of this example, the functionalist approach moves towards explaining the process of sifting experience and relating it to memory, responding to things in the present on the basis of my experience of the past. I've tasted that before, didn't like it then, so won't eat it now: functionalism offers a common-sense view of what we all do all of the time.

Relating to the rest of the world involves a whole range of mental phenomena that the nineteenth-century Austrian philosopher Franz Brentano described in terms of "intentionality". Willing, hoping, loving, hating: these activities are directed to something outside ourselves; they cannot happen without being "about" something; they refer beyond themselves. The object of their attention need not exist physically – I could be in love with a fantasy – but the intentional stance is real and is the mark of intelligent life. In 1890, the philosopher and psychologist William James described it in this way in the first chapter of his *The Principles of Psychology*:

> *The Pursuance of future ends and the choice of means for their attainment, are thus the* mark and *criterion of the presence of mentality* in a phenomenon. We all use this test to discriminate between an intelligent and a mechanical performance. We impute no mentality to sticks and stones, because they never seem to move for *the sake of* anything, but always when pushed, and then indifferently and with no sign of choice. So we unhesitatingly call them senseless.

It is likely, therefore, that the broad area of "intentionality" holds the key to how we develop as persons in our interaction with the world around us, but for now let us return to the issue of materialism.

Of course, the study of consciousness has come a long way since James's day, and the discussion of minds and brains is now set against a background of the cognitive sciences, where biology combines with psychology, linguistics and computer studies to explore the general ways in which our brains (seen very much as computers) relate to the world and create the experience of free, thinking, planning individuals. Indeed, as Dennett explained in an autobiographical article (2008), his aim was both to do philosophy and also to defend a specific empirical theory of consciousness. The question remains as to whether any scientific theory, since it is based on empirical evidence that needs to be tested and evaluated, is actually about "me" in the sense that we are to explore it.

However broad the context within which it is presented, the extreme materialist view that the mind is identical to brain activity makes exactly the same sense as saying that a Van Gogh painting is made up of trillions of tiny particles of paint and nothing else. The essence, significance and reality of a work of art cannot be revealed by the analysis of paint and canvas. Phenomena – whether observed or simply experienced inwardly – have a scale and arena within which they operate. Given an incorrect scale, they make no difference, and effectively they do not exist. A Van Gogh does not exist at a level of paint particles. Likewise, any explanation of human consciousness and self-awareness works at a level other than that of individual neurons.

This is illustrated by another major problem for the materialist view: our experience of freedom. If everything in the universe, including our brains is part of a causally determined mesh of physical particles, there seems to be no room for freedom, spontaneity or actions based on feelings and intuitions. Everything, it would seem, is pre-determined and externally caused. My freedom, indeed my experience of myself, is an illusion.

From the strictly scientific point of view, the idea of freedom is difficult to contemplate. Naturally enough, we do not understand all the causes that operate at any one time, but we assume that there will always be sufficient causes, and one day we may find them. Where we appear to exercise freedom, it can therefore be assumed that, with hindsight, it should have been possible to predict every single choice. And it's no good trying to cheat at this: the sudden decision to change one's mind is as predictable as the more obvious first decision.

John Searle, in *Freedom and Neurobiology* (2007), suggests that this gap between the experience of freedom and the assumption of determinacy will one day be resolved through a developing understanding of neurobiology. If we can frame the question about our experience of freedom carefully enough, it will one day be possible to examine it using scientific, empirical methods. None of this rings true to me. Even if there is a level of quantum indeterminism that accounts for freedom, this does not solve the problem; it merely pushes it into the future when science will know more than at this moment. Quantum indeterminacy might argue for an element of randomness at the heart of our neurologically controlled actions, but it cannot argue that our experience of freedom is, at bottom, the result of random determination. Why not? Because the experience of freedom is exactly the experience of weighing options, considering benefits or harm to be achieved, considering preferences. It is the point at which I, as an experiencing subject, can choose and thereby make a real difference in the world. The experience of freedom is not of a tiny indeterminate gap within which my freedom can act, but of a massive open goalmouth of freedom, with determining factors trying to stop me shooting in the direction I wish, like defenders in a football match. Sometimes I am frustrated in my quest for freely chosen action; sometimes I succeed in scoring. But I cannot see how we can honestly disclaim all responsibility for our overall choices in life. Pleading hormones, upbringing and economic circumstances will only get us so far when our choices have been judged unwise and land us in trouble; pleading neural activity will make little difference.

Imagine a situation in which you are offered a new job that is challenging, well paid and interesting, but involves long hours and requires you to move house, causing problems for your partner and a shift in school for your children. You've always wanted this job, but you love the place where you live now, and think of the friends from whom you'd be separating yourselves. Your act of free choice is thus hedged about with a growing number of factors. And the more you think about them, the more they grow. What were the messages about home and family with which you grew up? Who might have inspired you to better yourself and establish your career? The number of influences spreads outwards in the present and backwards into your past. And there are many other people involved, all of whom have their own sets of values, interests and influences. Where do you stop? How can you ever know that you've taken everything into account when coming to your decision? This dilemma was referred to by Martin Heidegger as the "infinite background" problem: every choice implies an inexhaustible number of background influences. And it's more complex than that, for those factors are constantly changing. In short, if we try to take everything into account, we will sink into a swamp of causes. In the end, we draw a line and simply jump one way or the other; we cannot weigh pros and cons any more or we will go mad. Hindsight may prove the decision to have been unwise, but in practice a choice has to be made.

Freedom in this situation is recognizing that certainty is never possible. It is recognizing and taking responsibility for a choice that cannot take everything into account. It cannot simply be the product of a mechanical process. We may search our neural databases until our brains hurt, desperately trying to weigh things up, but in the end no final answer is achievable, and we are forced to jump one way or the other.

Nobody can doubt that the functioning of the brain has a crucial factor in making us who we are. One has only to contemplate the sad reality of someone suffering from advanced dementia to see how fast the personality degenerates when the brain refuses to function properly. It is also, of course, true that one's thoughts and feelings are susceptible to drugs that directly affect the brain. Equally, a thought can plunge us into despair or elate us; the recognition of something welcome and familiar can trigger off bodily sensations of pleasure and warmth. Body and mind interact: we are both, and it seems clear that neither can be properly understood without the other. But that does not mean that the self can be *identified* with the brain. Materialism doesn't start to address the questions you might want to ask about the meaning and purpose of your life. If you feel confused, or sense that life is devoid of meaning or direction, having a neuroscientist tell you that it is all to do with activity in your cerebral cortex does not actually solve your problem. For philosophy

YOU THINK YOU ARE BODY EVERY SELF?

to address issues about life and living, it must be capable of interpreting and illuminating the process of thinking and choosing in a way that makes a difference for us. If it doesn't, it is little more than an intellectual indulgence.

As soon as we start to think about our own identity, a whole raft of questions appear. If my body gets old and decrepit, my career fails, my family falls apart and my friends desert me, am I the same person? Those things appear to define me, but are all liable to change. Clearly, I sense myself – including the inner voice that is most distinctively me – as inhabiting my head. Indeed, it is a fundamental fact of life that the perspective we have on the world comes from a point between and behind our eyes. We sense that we look out from that point. But reflect for a moment on the apparently empty space behind your eyes. You know very well that behind the soft jelly of your eyeballs there lie bony sockets, and behind them your brain, soft, grey, alive and energy-hungry. But you cannot see your own brain, nor can you be aware of its operations; all you sense is the world out there in front of you. But how do these experienced qualities, of colour, or shape, or texture ("qualia", to use philosophers' usual term for them), relate to the world outside and to the brain within? Are you seeing the world as it is, or an image of the world that is being digitally screened in your head? You know, when watching a film on screen, that what you are seeing is a flat matrix of coloured pixels, yet the impression is of looking through the television or computer screen as though it is a window on to a world behind. Might our own perception of the world be thought of in the same way: as a representation within the brain that gives the illusion that what we are seeing is somehow outside ourselves?

Many of the discussions of qualia fail to recognize the origins of experience. Something "out there" appears to be red. The experience of red, as mediated to the cerebral cortex through the retina and optic nerve, in the form of electrical impulses within neurons, *is* our experience of red. There is no hidden cinema in our brain that screens

16

a red image. And so, when we remember that colour, or talk about it, or see it again, *that colour is what we see.* When we look at the brain from an external point of view, there is no "red" to be seen.

I take a tin of tomatoes to the checkout at a supermarket. The label on the tin – a suitable tomato, red in colour – has been given a number and a barcode. At the till, the barcode is read and transmitted to the screen, which shows that I have bought the tin of tomatoes. If the checkout were really fancy, it might conceivably show a picture of the tin on the screen. The transmission of the information from scanner to bill is done in digital form. But that digital sequence can be read out as a tin of tomatoes, simply because it has been originally programmed as a tin of tomatoes. If I see red, I get red, and that's all there is to it. True, analysis of my neurons will not reveal something resembling a colour (any more than the analysis of the checkout will show me the colour of a tomato can), but the colour out there in the world is equally elusive. Can you really appreciate the shades represented by particular frequencies of light? The analysis of the light waves entering your eyeball is no more red than the pulses on the optic nerve. You have a sensation of red, because red is how you describe the sensations you receive.

There is a second way of coming at the same phenomenon; namely, by recognizing that experience and explanation are very different things. If I feel sexually attracted towards someone, I do not experience that as the promptings of my hormones; I simply experience the inclination that the hormones prompt. So we should not dismiss the materialist point of view simply because brain activity, externally observed, does not seem to be like the sensations it is tracking.

Materialists oppose any idea of a "ghostly" self working alongside the body, or initiating my inner monologues. The term used (in a very pejorative sense) by some American philosophers is "spook stuff". They argue that there is only one kind of stuff in the universe and that it is physical. But the idea of the self as a "ghost" came from

Ryle's *The Concept of Mind*, in which he caricatured what he then saw as the "official", dualist view of the relationship between mind and matter as "the ghost in the machine". Sadly, in philosophy as in many other spheres of life, caricatures are more memorable than historical characters, and just as a politician will gradually start to look more and more like his cartoon image, so theories can start to be summarized by their caricature. That has been the sad fate of Descartes's view of the relationship between mind and body, which is too often seen only through Ryle's logical behaviourist eyes.

René Descartes famously declared "I think, therefore I am". He was battling against scepticism, and this statement was the result of applying the principle of systematic doubt to everything that, in the ordinary course of events, he would have taken for granted. His senses may sometimes deceive him, so he assumes they always will. He cuts away all the regular certainties, until he reaches the one thing that he cannot doubt – namely, that he is a thinking being – for the very act of doubting requires thought. And that's where all the trouble starts, for the implication of his conclusion seems to be that mind and matter are utterly different things, and that the relationship between them is problematic.

While the body was physical, extended in time and space, Descartes argued that the mind was non-physical and non-extended. Unlike Ryle's caricature, Descartes never argued for any "ghost", for that would have been to imply that the mind existed *alongside* matter. Rather, the mental is for him something utterly different, not extended in space and therefore not part of the ordinary chain of physical causation that we observe in all material objects. But this raises obvious questions: if the mind is utterly different from physical matter, how can it make a difference in the physical world? How can a non-material, non-located mind interfere with the chain of physical causation?

There have been some curious attempts to answer that question. The seventeenth-century philosopher Nicolas Malebranche considered that mind and matter were utterly different, and there-fore could not affect one another directly. In other words, he saw no way to bridge what later became known as Leibniz's Gap between mind and matter. Hence he devised a theory called "occasionalism". This is clearly the most logical but daft theory to be built on dualist assumptions. I recognize my friend and smile. My mind feels happy. My mouth and cheeks pucker up and my eyebrows rise in a sepa-rate and unrelated operation that forms part of the causally condi-tioned world. My smile cannot be caused by my feeling happy, but – bringing in a deity to help overcome the problem – Malebranche would argue that, on the occasion of my feeling happy, God carried out a physical operation that produced the smile, so that feeling and smile could be synchronized.

Of course, when I said "I'm sorry, I was miles away" I implied a kind of dualism: that my body was present at the table, but my mind had wandered. And the instinctive thing was to identify myself with the mind, rather than with the body. Hence there is always going to be a natural inclination to interpret our experience in dualist terms. But where does that lead? Out of the original context in his quest for certainty, Descartes's quote becomes emblematic of the view that my true self, the "me" to which I alone have access, is my mind, distinct from and only tentatively linked to the body. The assumption was made that we are essentially thinking beings, trapped within physical bodies. The real "me" is private, special and unobserved; others only see my packaging, not the goods within.

There are a good number of reasons why people might opt for dualism as an explanation of the relationship between mind and body. Here are just some of them. If your "real" self is private and unobservable, you can always pretend to yourself that you are rather better, more clever and sensitive, than your external appearance and life in the outside, observable world would suggest. Nobody can ever really understand you (thank goodness!). There is also the obvious fact that the physical body is not the kindest thing with which to identify yourself. Old age is not pretty, for a start; but nor is adolescence. What one person may see as beautiful, another will experience as being the wrong shape. We are also vulnerable to the failure of our physical systems. Another understandable reason for opting for dualism is that it leaves open the possibility of some kind of survival of death. If my mind is not physical, why should it die with the body? Why should the soul not be eternal and move from one body to another?

But, if taken in a literal and crude sense, there will always be problems with separating off the thinking self from its physical body. How could a "soul" or self express itself without a body? How could it relate to other people? How, indeed, could it have any discernible character? If you are separate from your body, then I can never know the real you; I am isolated in a world of puppets, and have to assume the existence of unknowable mental puppeteers.

In the real world, however, we have multiple ways of assessing what another person is thinking and feeling (with or without the use of a polygraph lie detector). We assess another person by the sum total of all they say and do: their facial expressions, tell-tale grimaces or the fleeting twinkle of delight in the eye, body language and so on. We judge them over a period of time in different situations. We match up what they say with what they do, and the choices they make. The smile is a tool of social interaction; it not only reveals something about a person, but also establishes a bond. It may be true that we do not have direct awareness of other people's sensations – which is no surprise, since sensing is related to our own individual centre of consciousness – but that does not mean, for all practical purposes, that we cannot get a pretty clear idea of what they have experienced and of their motives for what they have done. If you don't believe me, go and read a detective story!

However, I think we can take a quite different approach to this matter of how minds and bodies are related. I think Descartes was mistaken in his identification of the self with the process of thinking, not because mind and matter are not radically different, but because of *what it is* that we think. Thinking is a tool, not a self; so let's look at what it does.

There is a radical difference between what you *think* and what you *are*. Thinking generally deals *with what you are not*. You see something and think "I'd like to buy that". You express an intention. But that intention relates to what is not at present the case. Thinking is, more often than not, about planning, sorting out, deciding what to do, establishing values. It looks at what is and asks if it could be different. That box is tightly shut: how do I open it? This business needs reorganizing: how do I set about radically altering it? This attractive person does not know me: how do I try to make him or her my friend? This job is boring: how do I change the work I do?

The process of thought is therefore one of either expressing – to yourself or to others – what you feel, in which case it is not the thinking that is primary, but the emotions that need to be expressed. Or it's a matter of deciding what to do, in which case the process of thought looks at what does not now exist – the various possibilities that are open to you – and tries to weigh up the pros and cons of each option. Or it's a matter of sorting out and clarifying shared ideas (as happens, most clearly, at a business meeting where those round the table are brainstorming a problem). In each case, thinking is an *agent*, a process that enables us to achieve something that is motivated by emotions, or a sense of personal values, or a shared enterprise. Thinking is an aid to living, a tool to help us to decide between courses of action, to warn us about possible consequences.

It would be very sad if people's emotions were entirely determined by their rational thoughts. They would be cold and potentially manipulative, every expression of affection the result of a calculation. For a thoughtful human being, however, emotions may rightly be examined and challenged. We can compare our intellectual grasp of values with our experienced emotions, so that the process of thinking can assess whether those emotions are a genuine expression of ourselves, or whether they are a superficial indulgence.

The idea that we are basically thinking beings that happen to inhabit physical bodies is only tenable for as long as we feel fit and well. When illness strikes, the mind is dulled, and all our awareness is of the pain, or the giddiness, or the raging fever, or whatever else it is that is afflicting us. At that moment, we sense that we are fully in our bodies, although the mind, when it rouses itself to clear thought, wishes that we were not linked to this source of pain.

There is only one world. Some things within it become conscious: a feature of the complexity of their bodies and their relationship with their environment. They sense and go for food, they protect themselves, they band together for protection. And as the process of consciousness becomes itself more complex, there is the phenomenon of reflective self-consciousness: not just being an "I" that is the centre of a set of experiences, but a "me" of reflective awareness. And from that point there builds the whole edifice of thought, so that the world is no longer just physical, but also valued and related to the sensing "I"; it takes on a new layer of reality – the mental layer. Everything is seen as physical and, at the same time, as interpreted in terms of meaning, purpose and value. It is that interpretation, related directly to the experiencing self, that forms the world of the mind.

Philosophy, as a way of addressing the art of living, uses reason to harness energy, intuition and desire to impact on our lives. Of all the options open to us, it advises on the most worthwhile, or the most likely to achieve our chosen ends. Thinking is about making a difference. That task will not be aided by a complete analysis of the brain, differentiating the various parts by function. That is an interesting quest in itself, but it is not our quest. In fact, having a complete analysis of the operation of my brain will no more change my understanding of "me" than the discovery of the Higgs boson (if the Large Hadron Collider at CERN achieves its intended purpose) will change my sense of wonder at the universe. A full body scan tells you what is going on but does not in itself improve your health; a course in car mechanics does not improve your driving; an omniscient neuroscience will not sort out the problem of being an individual or choosing what is worthwhile in life.

In Mary Shelley's novel, Frankenstein's "monster" had a problem. Artificially constructed and fired into life, the monster finds that he cannot relate to society. He has feelings but no outlet for them. He recognizes himself as an unnatural creation, condemned to isolation, and rebels against his maker. Yet, I sense that a narrowly interpreted materialist approach to the self makes a fundamentally Frankenstein-like mistake. It assumes that we are like machines that, once assembled and running, each part performing its own function, will explain in mechanical, electrical or chemical terms the world of relationships and all that we understand by human life. But the materialist creation will always remain a monster. A real person develops within a particular situation, with relationships and experiences that all contribute to the growing sense of self. That cannot be explained as the *product* of neural activity; it is the reaction to life's experiences. True, the brain will be remembering and weighing up one experience against another, but it will not be the *initiator* of that process.

The self is always real and embodied. Without that, our common experience of life makes no sense. But that does not mean that either side of the dualism–materialism debate has the whole answer. Neither does justice to the way in which I respond to the world around me, nor the way in which my understanding of myself is of a being who is embodied and always living in relationship to my surroundings. Whatever I am, I am trying to deal with the world around me. So where does that leave "me" at this point?

Personally I don't find either the materialist or the dualist approaches entirely satisfactory, and reckon that, when two incompatible answers are equally logical but equally unsatisfactory, it is a possible indication that the wrong question is being asked, or that the logic that sees them as mutually exclusive may be wrong. For example, following the philosopher Benedict Spinoza, it may be that the physical and the mental are the outer and inner aspects of the same phenomenon, the one giving the point of view of an observer, the other experienced by the subject self. Such a view might encompass key strengths of both the materialist and dualist approaches. Clearly, the materialists have a valid point. There is no place in the material world for something else, some "spook stuff" that is mind rather than body. There is no empty space behind my eyes from which I view the world; there is only bone and brain. But I am convinced that, when I refer to "me" or when I encounter "you", I am talking about a person, rather than a collection of neurons with body attached. Dualism at least matches the common-sense experience of being a self, with the inner dialogue and points of view that make each of us unique.

None of this, of course, detracts from the stunning phenomenon of the brain and what it achieves. With at least 100 billion neurons, the brain is by far the most complex thing we know in the universe. Already, neurobiology can set out the activities of its various parts: the amygdala coordinating our emotional reactions; the brain tissue, extending into the retina of the eye, transmitting messages back via the thalamus to the cerebral cortex to give us sight; the basal ganglia controlling our movements; the hippocampus storing long-term memories; and so on. It is quite amazing what the brain achieves, receiving signals and giving out instructions. Everything we do is mirrored in brain activity. In terms of our sense of ourselves – quite apart from running our physical systems and enabling us to respond to what is detected by our senses – we know that the brain processes and interprets our experiences and selectively remembers them. None of that is in doubt. But there remain fundamental questions about how brain activity relates to my own consciousness and the experience that I have of being "me".

There is still a huge gap between what neurobiology has revealed and the experience of being a human individual.

By the end of this book I hope to have persuaded you that there is a direct and obvious link between the way your brain handles memory, emotions and spatial awareness and the experience you have of being "you". But first we need to look at the way the mind goes about its task.

2. The mind goes hunting

Watch a newborn baby. Moments after birth, snuggling up against her mother's breast, she instinctively opens her mouth to receive the offered nipple and starts to suckle. She already knows what she needs and, finding it, is content. Even in those early stages of life, the baby takes a proactive stance towards her world. She cries out, drawing attention to herself, demanding to be taken notice of. At a very basic level, her mind is already responding to the world and interacting with it. Feelings and responses interlock perfectly: the baby needs milk and cries out; the nursing mother may start to produce breast milk at the sound of her baby crying.

Back in the seventeenth century, John Locke argued in his *Essay Concerning Human Understanding* that all knowledge comes through sense experience, and that we are born *tabula rasa*: a passive blank slate on which experience can start to write. But in actual fact, as anyone knows who has watched over a baby during his or her first days and weeks of life, pointers to what we shall become are already there at our birth. Babies have a personality out of all proportion to their experience. We are born with a genetic make-up that will shape our future, moulding us to become like our parents. We arrive in this life at a particular moment, in particular circumstances. We are, as Heidegger said, "thrown" into life; we cannot escape our inheritance. Think how different our lives would be were we to have been born to different parents in a different age or into a different culture. Two things are certain from the moment of our birth: the first is that we inherit more than we might have chosen; the second is that we do not wait to receive experience but go hunting for it. From the moment of birth, we are aware of what we lack, and set about finding what we want: a breast; a place to be cooler or warmer than we are now; a nappy that is clean and dry. A baby may express a preference for a particular position for sleep, one hand raised, or curled up, or stretched out. The mind of the tiny baby is not at all the blank slate that Locke imagined. It is far more like an interactive whiteboard. It doesn't just receive impressions but looks for them and relates to them. The baby is already starting to map out her personal world, and within a few weeks will begin to recognize faces and become used to the routine of her day. Give her another few months and the baby will be looking around, examining things, putting them into her mouth, touching, stroking, smiling (first at almost anything that is vaguely like a head, later at recognized faces), and generally expressing a whole range of attitudes. She quickly learns how to operate her world for her own benefit: when to smile and be quiet, when to yell in protest. The world is not simply a sequence of experiences waiting to be filed away in some great database in the brain; it is a lived environment. And with each new experience comes a set of values: this is pleasant or unpleasant, something I want more of, or something to avoid. It's not that babies are innocent, it's just that their vulnerability makes us sympathize with their egocentricity and go along with their manipulative demands.

But before we continue to follow the development of a sense of self in our baby, let us step back for a moment and contemplate the place that mental activity has within the overall shape of evolution. At the most basic level, things are inanimate and inert. A nail waits to be hammered; it does not wince and try to get out of the way once it sees the hammer coming. But even the word "wait" here is inappropriate, for waiting is a phenomenon of those creatures that are aware of the succession of events. The nail knows nothing. But we should not too quickly dismiss the inanimate, physical level in our survey of the human self, because once analysed into our component parts, each one of us becomes a collection of inanimate objects. We comprise atoms; below the cellular level, all signs of consciousness and life disappear. There is no part of us that is not, at one and the same time, part of the inanimate universe. And, to put it into an even broader perspective, there is no part of us that was not at one time part of something else, and long after we have departed this life, our atoms will be spread elsewhere. Our life is, at one level, a very temporary collection of inanimate things.

Life appears once a being reaches the point of being able to move, to feed and excrete and to reproduce. The simplest virus does this very effectively, as we know to our cost. Beyond that, in the evolutionary process, we reach the level of consciousness, a basic feature of all sentient beings whereby they are able to relate to the world, find their way around, feed and mate. But what distinguishes human beings from other species (as far as we are aware) is their ability to be aware of and reflect on their consciousness. Reflexive self-consciousness is the point of being aware of the process of willing and choosing, of seeking goals and avoiding threats. At a very basic level, my infant step-grandson is already displaying self-consciousness: he knows what he feels, and he knows whether something is happening to change those feelings. He is aware of contentment, and remembers enough to know where content-ment is to be found. The process of introducing him to new foods, or to a bottle rather than a breast, quickly illustrates his ability to decide which of the options he prefers, and he loses no time in deploying the standard means of protest in order to make his pref-erence known. A mouth clamped shut when offered one foodstuff is eagerly opened to receive another.

But the "I" that does the choosing, whether in a baby or in an adult, is a very strange thing. "I" is the focal point of my experi-ence; it is that which experiences, not part of what is experienced. Nobody can understand what it is to be the "I" that I am when I act. The "I" is not part of the world, but the point from which I view the world. In his *Tractatus Logico Philosophicus*, written in 1921, Ludwig Wittgenstein described the self as the "limit" of the world. Nobody else can understand what it is to experience and think as I do, for "I" am not part of the world they experience, nor part of the world that I can describe effectively, for as soon as I turn inwards to look at myself, I start to describe parts of "me" as though from an *external* point of view. But that is not the same as the experience I myself have as I express preferences, make decisions, fall in love, experience fear, hunger, elation or awe. In every act of thinking and choosing, I am essentially a constructor, a fabricator: I am making something that I can also describe as "me".

One of the most significant turning points in Western philosophy came when Immanuel Kant proposed his "Copernican revolution" in the way we experience the world. Just as Copernicus had argued that the earth revolved around the sun, rather than the other way round, so Kant argued that the most basic features of the world as we experience it – space, time and causality – were not to be found "out there" in the world, but were imposed on our experience by our minds. In other words, Kant recognized that the mind played an active role in shaping our experience of the world. The world we know is "our" world, and it appears the way it does simply because that is the way our senses are devised to understand it. What it was like in itself, he believed, remained unknowable.

After Kant, other philosophers explored the way in which the creative activity of the mind shaped our experience of the world. Ludwig Feuerbach argued that God was not an external, objective reality, but a projection of humankind's highest aspirations. The great sweep of G. W. F. Hegel's philosophy embraced the changing features of the world as part of an overall intellectual scheme, each expressing the spirit of its age. Friedrich Nietzsche, recognizing the loss of traditional values in the mid-nineteenth century, threw down the challenge of setting one's sights on the future and establishing new values. In the great sweep of evolution, human-kind was something to be overcome in striving forward to establish the *Übermensch*, or superman, who would embody the meaning of the earth. And in the twentieth century, the existentialist trad-ition, which we shall examine later, took up this theme, giving the individual a responsibility for shaping and creating his or her own essence. These and other philosophers point to the way in which the mind creates and gives value to the experienced world. The mind takes the ongoing feed of experience from the sense organs and assesses it, rejects that which is irrelevant, becomes acutely attuned to that which is more important, and starts to build up a map of its own world, a map that shows it how to live, how to operate, how to get satisfaction, how to avoid danger.

The baby is already an "I", but is only at the very start of the process of becoming aware of himself or herself as a "me". But, being crea-tures endowed with the possibility of reflexive self-consciousness, we are soon able to reflect on what it is that the mind finds, and on the significance of the fact that it goes looking in the first place. Very early on, the child will recognize that he or she has a place within the scheme of things. When it comes to being picked up, she starts to prefer its parents to strangers. She gets more clingy, as the reality of her "me" begins to dawn and with it the sense of her own vulnerability. She starts to seek out predictable coordinates for her life and sees herself as living within a world of other beings, no longer confident of being the centre of things.

A tiny baby appears to be aware only of her own personal feelings and needs. At six months old, she is sitting up and looking around, orientating herself in a world that contains other people. And that personal world grows; we find ourselves becoming a member of a playgroup, or a school, of a university, career, state, global interest group. I am aware of being a "me" in those contexts. As adults, we know that, when people describe "me" they are not describing what it is like to experience as I experience: they are describing my place in the various networks and patterns that surround me. I am who I am because of everyone else: a claim used in a recent advertising campaign to sell, appropriately enough, mobile communications.

To explore the reality of "me" we can therefore expand our enquiry to include those things that shape or express our personalities, from the personas we might adopt as avatars in cyberspace, to the profiles that advertisers need in order to target us to buy their products. There is the "me" that Nietzsche described as always striving to become something more, or that Jean-Paul Sartre saw as creating meaning and acting in good or bad faith. Indeed, a key feature of the existentialist approach to the self is that one does not have a fixed essence but constructs the self through the process of living, as when Simone de Beauvoir famously declared, "One is not born, but rather becomes, a woman". So the active, engaged, responding mind starts to mould the features of my personality, but also, in its engagement with the world, it creates an objective, visible "me" that other people can see and relate to.

There is a danger here. The "me" that appears objectively out there in the world may not be quite as good as "I" wish it to be. I may be convinced that I can do more, be more, achieve more. How do I appear to others? Do they have the right impression of me? Am I to them what I appear to myself? I may be tempted to say that nobody understands "the real me". Reality may lag behind aspiration, getting in the way of my dreams; I may distance myself from the "me" that is out there in the world, doing its mundane job, trying to establish itself and nurture relationships, just because the "real me" is so much nicer, more successful, more creative. The danger is that we can separate off the fantasy ideal "me" from the actual "me" and believe that the former is more real than the latter. That way lies madness.

But what is happening on the neural front while I am developing my personal sense of "me"? The sense organs are feeding information to the brain, and in turn are being informed by it. Everything is evaluated as pleasant, painful or neutral and is related to past experience. The brain builds up a network of associations, uniquely informed by all that is available to our memory. It finds and works on patterns of significance and thus confers meaning to the new stream of experience. Without memory and past experience, we would seem lost in an utterly unfamiliar world.

This is a constantly changing, evolving process, not some mechanical filing of data into a database. But its recognition is not new. In 1890, William James published *The Principles of Psychology*. It is an amazing book, in which he examines very specifically what we consider to be "me", and is quite prepared to speak of the different worlds within which we encounter things, recognizing that things will appear quite different within the world revealed by science from how they appear in the world of common experience, or that of values, or aesthetic appreciation. It is one of those classic books that touches on so many relevant issues that it is difficult to believe (other than by the quality of its language and the discursive nature of its argument) that it was published in the nineteenth century. In it he makes the point that our consciousness is not a "thing" but a "process", one that is private, selective, continuous and changing. We develop as persons through the ever-changing stream of consciousness.

But let us return again for a moment to our early years, and take a look at a major element in our inheritance. If I stub my foot, topple over or hit my head, I may well (depending on my frame of mind and degree of surprise at the mishap) express myself by way of an expletive, or at least say something of the fact that I regret what has happened. And I'm likely to do that whether or not there is anyone else within earshot; indeed, I may well look round to check, with some relief, that nobody has heard me. When she first hurts herself, the baby looks shocked and then cries, but she cannot speak, cannot even think in words. She has no vocabulary with which to express herself. Imagine for a moment what you will never be able to remember: those first pre-linguistic months. Whatever you do now, you have an inner dialogue running through your head. You comment to yourself. Even at the moment when you let fly an expletive, you may almost simultaneously find a voice in your head saying that you shouldn't really have said that, and that you should check that nobody has heard you. Imagine a world in which you have no such inner dialogue, because you have no concepts, no way of defining and expressing your responses to what happens. In such circumstances, all you can do is squawk even louder.

That, of course, is because the baby has not yet received what she will soon start gathering in at a huge rate: her linguistic and cultural inheritance. Even if we agree to some extent that we are born as an interactive version of Locke's *tabula rasa*, we cannot deny that we will only start to express ourselves when we have started to inherit and use the vast world of language and ideas. The words we use are provided for us by our environment. We would not learn to speak if others did not speak to us. Our native language is the one we learn from those around us. Were we to have been born elsewhere, our native language would have been different. Our thinking is not really ours; it is borrowed. We do not have to learn everything from scratch with each generation. Along with our genetic make-up, we inherit all that has gone before us, originally mediated by words and explanatory actions, then by reading what those before us have written, or watching television, or surfing the internet. Nowadays we become immersed in a world of words and images that is truly global, and through which we have to pick our way selectively if we are to retain any manageable sense of who we are. For each of us is born at a time, into a culture and a language, into an economic and political system, into a family and community structure, that will, over the years, mould our thoughts and aspirations. It will provide us with a set of values that we may cheerfully adopt or consciously reject. It will make assumptions about what we should do and how we should behave. Even the most individualist and creative people arrive into a ready-made environment and start to go along with it or react against it. You only know what you want when you know what you don't want: when you realize that there are choices to be made.

But as we have already seen, we are thrown into the particular circumstances of our life, and we immediately get on with doing what which is expected of us. We do not always have the luxury of standing back and questioning our linguistic or social heritage. There is a significant part of our minds that appears to be hard-wired to enable us to function in society. And this, of course, has implications for evolution. Whereas some biologists – see, for example, Richard Dawkins's argument in *The Selfish Gene* (1976) – consider the process of natural selection as happening primarily at the level of individuals, Edward Wilson examines evolution in terms of group selection, and has made a particular study of ants. It is clear that ants are born for a clearly defined social purpose. All they see and know is conditioned by the needs of the ant community. Ant colonies are constantly at war with one another and therefore each colony needs to demand absolute loyalty of its members. The social hard-wiring therefore allows colonies to succeed and thus the species to evolve by using the advantage given by the most efficient social control and interaction. Successful individuals, from this point of view, cannot contribute to the future if they go down because the society that supports them fails. Individual success depends on effective social networking.

So, if you're an ant, you are not born *tabula rasa*. You do not wait to find out what would be in your own interest or that of the group and then decide how to act. You are born with a role and a set of values; it is a given. What then of humans? Wilson conceives that it is possible to see social functions (including religion) as giving a biological advantage. We may like to think we are superior to the ants. We are free. But to what extent is that true? How much of what we become in life is governed by events and attitudes that were around before our birth? Can we be genuinely original – a total one-off – or are we mostly following in a tradition, in inherited genes? Without doubt, we experience freedom, and it is therefore easy to say that we cannot possibly be like ants. But we cannot know what it is like to be an ant. We may assume that our increased brain size gives us the ability to reflect on our situation in a way that an ant cannot, but can we be sure that the ant does not simply feel inclined to do what it needs to do? And are we sure that our apparent freedom is not determined largely by hormones, genetics and social conditioning?

The idea of a human being as a mechanism, to which is attached a mind that remains largely unknown to all but the experiencing subject, goes against our most obvious experience of life. In order to live we need to feed, to explore the environment, to create shelters against the elements. But our survival also requires cooperation and communication. The face has many and subtle ways of showing emotion, interest, boredom and so on. A nod, a wink, a sign, a raising of the eyebrows; all these communicate very effectively, and they are interpreted in context. At a more complex level, however, cooperation requires language and language implies thought. We think in order to live.

The fact that I am alive and conscious means that I relate to my environment; I experience things as pleasant or painful. Those sensations are taken and evaluated so that I know what situations to seek out and what to avoid. That process of sorting sensations gives the initial impetus to the mental life. The more sophisticated we become, the more mental processing we do. But that processing is nothing in itself: its context is the interplay between self and world. We think because we are alive. Being born into an environment in which we have to be discerning if we are to survive is the very reason for thought. For, as Aristotle said, man is a political animal. To be human – and certainly to live the good life – is to be connected and engaged. The life of the observer and consumer is sub-human. Indeed, language about the meaning of life generally implies shared goals, for most activities are only achievable within a social context and shared language and ideals. I could not write this book unless the publisher guessed that you might be willing to read it. Nor, of course, could the very idea of buying books and thereby sharing ideas be possible in a world where each individual lives in solipsistic isolation. And it is not merely language and grammar that need to be shared in order to engage in this reading and writing experience; there has to be a common interest in certain ideas and intuitions about life.

And it is the degree of shared language, concepts and experiences, and the need to cooperate in order to survive, that makes it so unrealistic to try to define "me" simply in terms of what is going on within my own head and body. In his *Essay Concerning Human Understanding*, Locke suggests that personal identity is "a native impression, and consequently so clear and obvious to us, that we must needs know it even from our cradles" (I.iv.4), but that it is not at all obvious how a constant self is compatible with a changing body over the course of its life. But the native impression of myself, however obvious, needs to take into account those things, beyond my body, of which I am conscious and with which I identify. This may include those shared concerns of which I am aware and in which I believe myself to have a personal stake. If I am conscious of them, they become part of me. Brain, body, home and family are the obvious points at which to start; but also career, nation, shared interest groups, indeed the whole sense of the human race living within a rather precarious but beautiful film of life over the surface of this planet. If you are conscious of it, it becomes part of what you understand by "me": part of your identity as a human person. So understanding ourselves will also require examining those external social and physical structures within which we operate.

Living comes first; thinking about living comes later. And that applies equally to the individual and to the development of humankind. One of the most fascinating books on the development of the human mind has the most intimidating title _The Origin of Consciousness in the Breakdown of the Bicameral Mind_. Written in 1976 by Julian Jaynes, it explores the origins of the process of self-reflective consciousness, the sense that we can have that inner dialogue, questioning our meanings and motives. He looks at the origin of consciousness in evolution, particularly starting with the period when the ancient Greek narrative of the _Iliad_ was being put together, a narrative that he traces back to about 1230 BCE. And what he shows (here in only the crudest caricature – please read the book itself, it is one of the finest for getting into these issues) is that at the time of the _Iliad_, there was no self-consciousness in the way we experience it now; no inner dialogue about what we might or should do. Confronted with an external challenge, the bicameral mind, as he calls it, simply waits for what is sensed as an external source of wisdom to give instructions. It is as though, at that phase of evolution, man did not question or think through what he should do, but waited for instructions from a deity.

He contrasts this with the _Odyssey_, composed over a period of time but a century or so later than the _Iliad_, in which Odysseus is depicted as self-motivated, cunning and crafty: in short, displaying all the traits of modern self-consciousness. He argues that, at a certain point in human evolution, therefore, the mind started to operate in a very different way. It became more self-aware, started an inner dialogue with itself, became conscious of its own consciousness. And from that moment, the characters that stride over the stage of literature have their own inner longings and plans, their own personal hopes, fears and tragedies. Before that time, they are presented as puppets, obedient to the deities but hardly self-aware. The meaning of life for the bicameral mind was given by external things; the meaning of life after the development of self-reflexive consciousness is developed within ourselves.

This shift is taken a step further in the European Enlightenment of the seventeenth and eighteenth centuries, when once again there is a focus on self-awareness and the autonomy of the individual. And so we are back where we started earlier in this chapter, with Kant and the idea of the mind that actively goes out to interpret experience. But before we assume too readily that the proactive mind – hunting, colonizing and interpreting what it experiences – knows what it's doing, we need to recognize that much of what makes us what we are comes from a depth that is below the conscious.

Plato did not subscribe to a *tabula rasa* view of the mind. He argued that our natural ability to understand abstract ideas goes beyond experience and therefore suggested that we arrive in this world pre-programmed to understand them. How is it, he asked, that a relatively untutored young person can so easily grasp mathematics? Clearly, there can never be enough experience to give certainty to abstract ideas of quantity; somehow the mind seems aware of perfection, and uses that to judge the particular things it encounters. One can imagine a perfect sphere, even if every sphere ever encountered is less that perfect. The idea – the perfect "form" – is the standard by which we judge. But where does that "form" come from? Plato explores the possibility that, before birth, we inhabit the eternal world of the Forms, and arrive in this world of imperfect copies ready programmed to start appreciating general terms and ideas. There are, of course, other ways of approaching this same issue of our collective inheritance. Jungian psychology, for example, refers to the archetypes: deeply imprinted cultural images that lead to self-understanding. As individuals, we do not construct these, but inherit them. For Jung, we have an inner life that is nourished all the time by symbols, images that are effective in promoting our own sense of significance. We understand the world through the archetypes.

So where does that get us? In this chapter I have argued that the mind is not a passive recipient of experience, and hence that the "me" that I refer to as my real self, that which lies behind the ever changing "I" that does my experiencing, is something that I am actively engaged in shaping. But where, as the mind actively inter-prets its experience and develops a sense of its own meaning, does it discover the images that promise satisfaction? What is worth doing in life? What should our goals be? What, in the end, can count as success in life? That is the question to which we now need to turn.

3. Roads to success?

So what counts as success? What counts as quality? When do we think of ourselves as having achieved our potential? And if the trajectory of our life reaches its highest point half way along, do we spend the first half of life looking forwards in anticipation, and the second half looking back with nostalgia or regret? Some might argue that the matter is simple; the image says it all. We see a product, an image, a dream: a bronzed, muscular hunk of a man; a shapely girl wearing innocently provocative clothes, simpering as she sips her drink; a happy family gathered around a table in awe at the meal the mother has produced instantly and cheaply – two for the price of one, on special offer, and all's well with the world. If the advertisement succeeds we say to ourselves, not just "I want to be like that!" but "I can be like that!", as we reach for our credit cards. And we do not even need to believe that an advertisement is making a serious life suggestion; humour works equally well. One image, in the weekend colour supplement of a quality newspaper, depicted a handsome man relaxing at the back of a speedboat, casually holding a bottle of water as his craft cut through the azure sea. At first glance, you do not see what product it might be selling. Boats? Swimwear? But then you spot in a lower corner the words "Serving suggestion" set alongside the label of that bottle of water. You laugh, and perhaps vow never to buy that brand of water, but the image has worked its magic; you do not forget it.

And so "me" becomes a commodity to be enhanced and flattered. The product placement to beat all others is "me" placed in the most seductive of situations, and available on credit, or by signing up, or by voting for the right party, or by going on a demonstration, or by achieving potential by taking a university course. We are always looking for roads that might lead us to success in the art of living.

The long-running *Teach Yourself* series of books, which recently celebrated its seventieth anniversary (itself an indication of just how deeply engrained is the urge to self-help, self-improvement, self-education) used the slogan "Be where you want to be" on its covers. That is the mantra of all self-help books: you can achieve your potential; you can choose your future. We all have this secret intuition that we are really only functioning with a small part of our potential; that somewhere there is the opportunity waiting to branch out, to discover hidden talents, to achieve the greatest success yet. And all this – this longing to do and be more – is deeply ingrained. We are aware always of our limitations. We seek to overcome them. We may or may not succeed.

Two subject areas flourish in bookshops: business titles and those in the "mind, body, spirit" section. These are two sides of a single coin and use much the same forms of language: setting goals for yourself; recognizing your own potential; setting a plan of action to get from where you are now to where you want to be; getting in touch with those sides of your personality that you will be able to mobilize in your task. This is the realm where "me" is king, where self-analysis and reflection are encouraged, where the perceived "me" can enlarge to match the aspirational "me", where there is no limit to the "me" I might become. All you need is to have the courage of your convictions.

The first assumption of all this literature is that, for most people most of the time, the experience of life is one of an unsatisfactoriness that they long to overcome. This analysis of the human condition is not new. In the sixth century BCE, the Buddha argued for three general features of existence as the starting-point of his philosophy: that all things change, that there is no fixed self and that life is generally experienced as unsatisfactory. This recognition of "unsatisfactoriness" (often misleadingly translated as "suffering") is the starting-point for any quest to find a more fulfilled life. If we believe, as a matter of principle, that everything is fine just as it is, then we have no motive to change. The Buddha's challenge, in the face of the philosophies of his day, which opted for either nihilism or a rigid and formal acceptance of the status quo, was to follow a path of self-development that involved intellectual, emotional and practical steps. If *Teach Yourself* books had been available in his day, the Buddha would have been the ideal author for *Teach Yourself the Roads to Success* or *Teach Yourself the Quest for Happiness*. Indeed, he might well have been offered a two book deal! His style of presentation – setting out the path to be taken in terms of systematic steps, with the principles of his philosophy presented in the form of easily remembered lists – was one that modern self-help books do well to follow.

Even if we mock the tone and the banalities that are offered in some modern quests for happiness and success, we still fall for it. In the back of our minds we may say "I'm above that", and yet, in doing so, we have fallen (albeit possibly at a higher level) into the same trap. We have looked at ourselves, and at others, and we have judged where we are in the scheme of things; we have asked about our selves, and have said not just "I can be more", but "I already am more". At that moment, we stand back from the subject self. We cease to see with clear vision because our eyes are already turning in their sockets as we consider our own status. What I do next is not simply the result of a creative urge; it is calculated to produce a response, to establish "me" where I wish to be.

As all those books on how to succeed in business will tell you, it is all about setting realistic goals and achieving them one by one, constantly reaffirming a positive message. But at management level there is another absolute rule: do not micromanage. Faced with an uncertain future, there is a constant tendency – whether it is within a senior management team of a company, or at board level – to spend too much time looking over the details of day-to-day operations, rather than debating longer-term strategies, values and goals. Companies can sometimes head nowhere with devastating effectiveness. Even a global banking system can go for unregulated growth that looks impressive as it powers forwards, but foolish when its bubble is finally pricked.

So, in understanding what it means to make a success of "me" we may find something to learn from the 2008/2009 global credit crisis. Failure, we are told, comes from lack of confidence: not lack of self-confidence (there has been rather too much of that in some quarters) but lack of confidence of others in us. In other words, it is important to match one's own perception of one's value with objective measures that are visible to others. Delusion occurs when one's own valuation does not match market worth. Perhaps, therefore, the best way to increase the market value of "me" is to set realistic personal goals and tick them off as they are achieved, checking each time that they are within the overall parameters that we have set for our lives. But sadly, as anyone who has run some-thing as straightforward as a business knows, to say nothing of the emotional complexities of running a human life, it's not that easy.

We may not all have delusions of grandeur, or aspire to universal fame, but, at a lower level, the striving to achieve more at least in some limited areas of life is a near-universal but often secret ambi-tion. It may, of course, be related to delusion about one's own abili-ties, and it may cause havoc, both to the individual concerned and to others. An obsessive can ruin his or her family life; the dreams of a dictator can be deadly. And yet, if natural selection does indeed work at the level of the individual, it might be thought that the aspi-ration to be greater, to be and to achieve more, or even to struggle to reach the age at which one can breed, is only part of that greater impulse of evolution, dominated by the most fundamental of biological urges. To be powerful, good looking, charming: yes, we know that is all down to sex. And yet to assume that it is all for the purpose of sex is to mistake vehicle for destination. The sex drive is a profound biological urge, simply because it is the way of continuing the species. The drive to be sexually attractive and therefore selectable as the partner of someone equally attractive is only its logical development. And the quest to be "more", when it comes to it, is a secondary feature of the basic quest to survive and breed.

So perhaps we should not mock the self-help, become-more, you-can-do-it mentality. However superficial and banal its recommendations on occasions, it touches the most fundamental of biological needs. And the self – the "me" that is shaped by all the ambitions that drive us and decisions we make – mirrors where we wish to be, rather than where we have come from. The "me" is always aspirational. But before we get too carried away with implementing the business plan that will deliver the future success of project "me", there are three things to consider: our infinite background, the way we relate as individuals to our social and physical environment, and our ability to understand what constitutes an objective measure of success.

Heidegger argued in *Being and Time* ([1927] 2008) that we are all "thrown" into life. We are born in a particular set of circumstances, and these give us the context within which we are required to make sense of our life. We may dream about a possible future, but – unless we are seriously deluded – we cannot dream about a possible past; we are who we are. What is more, there are at any one time an infinite number of things that impact on us and determine what we do. We can never give an exhaustive account of the causes of anything. This may be termed the "infinite background" problem.

Of course, language and ideas are based on concepts, and concepts are an abstraction from what we encounter in our concrete situation. So whatever dreams and goals we have, they are likely at any time to be knocked sideways by circumstances that are beyond our control, and which remind us that we are never able to free ourselves entirely from our infinite background of influences. One thinker who has explored the implication of this is Milan Kundera, particularly in his novel *The Unbearable Lightness of Being* (1984). A key theme (among others) in that book is the painful awareness that the shaping of our lives may depend on things that happen at random, make no sense, and yet provide circumstances within which we are forced to make decisions. Kundera makes the point that it is very difficult for us to accept that random events shape us, and that we therefore have no inherent significance. We either labour under the weight of our responsibilities and commitments, or we find that we float off unencumbered but at the mercy of change and chance, with no sense of significance or purpose. The Buddha once described life as the froth on the tip of a wave. We are no more than bubbles that try to take themselves seriously.

Whatever else we know, therefore, we know that we are born by chance into a particular set of circumstances, and that throughout life we will be pushed one way or another by chance events, and that finally we will die. Human life would appear to be a zero sum game, with much throwing of dice. How, then, can we take seriously the attempt to define our own success? Before addressing that question, we need to look at the second of our three prior considerations: the relationship between the individual and his or her background.

Little things make all the difference. Between me and every other human being most of the genetic code is held in common (and, embarrassingly enough for our more pretentious views of the human future, we hold most of it in common with all other living things, not just the higher apes). But it is the tiny variations that make me unique and enable me to be identified by my DNA. When it comes to finding our place in life, we need to feel that we are special, unique, different. We fear getting swamped, being treated impersonally; nothing is worse than the dehumanizing treatment of prisoners, whether in Guantanamo Bay or the Stalinist gulags. Ever since philosophy emerged in ancient Greece, and reinforced by the European Enlightenment, there has been a recognition that human beings are, and deserve to be treated as, unique individuals. We are not ants in our anthill, serving the promptings of our predetermined role. We want to be free to choose and shape who we are and what we do.

So on the one hand there is a very definite need to stand out from the crowd and be an individual. But on the other hand there is the fear of rejection, of being outcast. In uncertain situations we crave knowledge of what others do, of what is expected of us. If vulnerable, we need to blend into the background, act like the others, draw no attention to ourselves. Individuality may be splendid when we are in charge and all is well with the world; when the going gets tough we need the security of the herd. So the double aspect to the changing "me" – to conform and then to stand out – is exploited by advertisers, who know how to capitalize on that ambivalence. You, the consumer, are unique, special, valued, chosen to receive this offer. The product will make you special, define you, make you stand out from the crowd. But you know, even as you key in your credit card number, that thousands of others are doing exactly the same thing. You are all unique, all special, all following the crowd. You are thus encouraged to stand out from one group (the mass of unenlightened consumers) only to find yourself fully embedded in another (those discerning enough to select this product). Every free magazine sent by a motor manufacturer attempts to strengthen your brand loyalty, to make you feel that you are the sort of person who will automatically want to stay with that product. Having bought the car, you may not be able to afford the crewed yacht that is being advertised, but you would like to feel perhaps that you are the sort of person who might be able to buy it; or even that the people in the car showroom *assumed* that you were the sort of person who might do so. But stand out you must, and if an actor, writer or sportsperson cannot do so solely on the basis of creativity, then bad behaviour will serve just as well. Getting noticed is an effective way of establishing identity. Hence the feature of belonging to inter-locking circles: being a pop singer, and being in rehab, and being a victim of the paparazzi, and being investigated for tax irregularities, and owning a very special, secluded house in an area where there are other special, secluded houses.

So we have at least started to unpack two of the three issues that enable us to examine success and the possible roads to achieve it: awareness that our circumstances are given to us, and that random and chance events may at any moment distort (and perhaps end) our otherwise over-planned lives; and awareness of the way in which we understand ourselves as individuals who both need, and need to stand out from, the group. But now we should examine the third fundamental background question: are there objective criteria by which success can be measured?

There are two very different approaches to establishing values. One is to say that the values (and therefore the measures of success) by which we live should be those that we freely choose and create for ourselves. This approach looks at the physical universe around us and notes that values do not inhere in it. Value, purpose, meaning, success: these things are products of human engagement with the world, not features of the world itself.

David Hume points out in *A Treatise of Human Nature* (1739–40) that, in discussions about morals, people often start by saying what "is" the case, and then slip into saying what "should be" the case, moving without justification from facts to values. This slippage from facts to values, called the "naturalistic fallacy" by G. E. Moore in his *Principia Ethica* (1903), is a major issue for ethical thinking. If values are independent of facts – at least to the extent that they do not depend on them – then there is a tendency towards relativism. If the values I choose for my life are different from yours, there are no facts to decide between them or pronounce one inherently better than another. So one possibility, which is reflected in many self-help publications and is often justified in terms of the multicultural nature of society in the West, is that we all have the responsibility for deciding what we will do with our lives. The only success and failure we face is the very personal one of either living up to our personal goals or failing to do so. One person's success can be another person's failure, and all are as good as one another. The other approach, reflected both in ethics and in the philosophy of religion, is to attempt to establish certain features of life that can serve as objective standards of value. The "natural law" approach to ethics considers that human reason is able to examine and establish the place and purpose of each thing within the overall scheme of the universe. It asks whether there is an essential nature to human beings, and, if so, how it may be expressed. It suggests that, to be a success, one should fulfil one's own potential, and that potential is given to you, not created by you. It is the potential with which you are born.

But do we find or create our values? Nietzsche, in the opening of *Thus Spake Zarathustra* ([1883–5] 1961), presents the image of Zarathustra coming down from his mountain retreat to survey the world and marvelling that people did not realize that God was dead. He therefore throws down the remarkable challenge: "Man is something that should be overcome. What have you done to overcome him?" (Prologue, §3). Describing humankind as walking a tightrope between its animal past and its anticipated future, Nietzsche looks towards the ideal of the *"Übermensch"*, the "overman" or next stage in human evolution. Poorly translated as "superman", the *Übermensch* expresses the best of human aspirations. But this happens in a context that was set out in another of his remarkable images, presented in his book *The Gay Science* ([1882] 1991). A madman appears in the marketplace in broad daylight carrying a lantern. He declares that God is dead, that the world is becoming colder and darker, that the horizon has been sponged away, and that the earth has become unchained from its sun. And then he says the most chilling thing: "Is there still any up or down? Are we not straying as through an infinite nothing? Do we not feel the breath of empty space?" (§125).

In other words – and in one of those wonderful moments of insight in which Nietzsche sums up the whole shift of thinking of his generation – he saw that the world was moving away from the comfort of established, fixed values towards an unknown and darker future, in which it would be the responsibility of humankind to establish its own value, its own measure of success. Not an easy option, but a chilling one. The challenge presented by Nietzsche is to see humankind as something to be overcome, its higher goal expressed in terms of the *Übermensch*, the next move forward in the march of evolution. He argues, not that the superman *is* the meaning of the earth, but that one's will should declare that the superman *shall be* the meaning of the earth. We are to affirm what we shall become, establishing our own values. But all of that makes sense only once we experience that cold breath of empty space: the valueless, meaningless world from which the external guarantees and structures have been removed. We cannot make sense (or a success) of our lives without one of two conditions: either we believe that there remains an external, objective system of values and meaning (whether given by God, or simply existing within the universe); or we are committed to establishing a system of values by an act of will. If one is removed without the other being established, we are in despair.

But here there is a problem, illustrated again by Kundera's contrast of lightness and weight. If we accept that there are objective values to which we are able (and should) commit our lives, we labour under them and are weighed down by them. But nevertheless, we have a sense that the meaning and success of our lives is given, fixed by those external values. Many people have given their lives in the name of "freedom and democracy", "the socialist movement" or "God". Martyrs to causes, whatever those causes may be, achieve the ultimate measure of success, if value is objectively given. By contrast, if our sense of success is to be based on our own personally chosen values and projects, we are always open to being challenged. Our decisions have no weight, because no decisions have weight. Everything is as good as everything else, and to suggest otherwise is to be accused of elitism or intellectual snobbery.

So, mindful of these three background issues – the circumstances and random events that impact on us, the double need to be special and unique and yet to blend in, and the need to consider whether the goals to which we aspire are fabricated or found – we can perhaps now take a brief look at some of the possible roads to success open to us.

Friends and family are a favourite route. It does not matter how wealthy or poor you are, nor what work you do; the thing that is going to give you lasting satisfaction is your family, and your life will be valued best by those closest to you. Indeed, many an obituary of the great and good points to that person as having a happy family life, setting the seal on other achievements. That is, without doubt, a wonderful measure of success, but it is always vulnerable to the changes and chances of life. Starting with all the best intentions, relationships can go wrong; physical traumas from wars to disease can rob us of those whom we love; other people's choices may ruin our own plans and dreams.

Another popular route is via work. At least success in a career, business or profession is measurable. Artists, writers and musicians may see themselves valued in terms of the sales of what they produce, or their reviews (although that is the most dangerous of routes to take!). Or, failing that, they may see their value in terms of the appreciation of a minority of cognoscenti, and their failure to capture the public's attention becomes a sign that their sophistication is way beyond common taste. In business, success is a matter of money made, empires built, a reputation established in the market. Again, it is vulnerable. Many people define themselves by what they do, finding in the predictability of work a sense of direction and established value that they may not find so easily in the more ambiguous world of relationships and personal values.

Sport or the arts can offer an immediate and tangible sense of success. Taking part in any activity with others, sensing companionship and shared projects, is a great boost to self-esteem and a sense of purpose generally. The faces of the Olympic winners say it all: exhausted satisfaction; a sense of pride, in oneself and also in one's country; a sense of personal achievement; and the justification of all that effort of training. Here, surely, is a true measure of success. But here, too, there is a downside, for the hunger for success leads some to take drugs to improve performance. There is a fine line between the genuine striving to be the best, and a narrower selfishness that wants to win at all costs.

Then there's politics. Public service is a noble way of submerging one's own life within the flow of society and of effecting change for the better. A sense of civic duty, and the recognition of Aristotle's claim that man is a political animal, promises to make the political route a worthwhile one. Although notoriously fickle, the political arena offers real measures of success, whether at the ballot box or in terms of government legislation or running a ministry. Public recognition gives the semblance of objective valuation.

But notice what all these things have in common. They all retreat from establishing some overall measure of success, and instead settle for a limited sphere of operation within which the measures of success can be more clearly defined. Notice also that they are overlapping. A politician may – famously – claim to be leaving government in order to spend "more time with his/her family". Some assume that to be an excuse to mark frustration or failure, but it may also be genuine. There is a balancing act to perform here: family life, career, sport and political engagement may all find their place in terms of a well-balanced life. Perhaps, like an investor placing funds, it is safe to spread widely across the market, so that failure in one area may be compensated for by success in another. So we tend to admire the person who handles different aspects of life with equal enthusiasm and overt success: the mother of four who is also a successful city trader; the scientist who is an accomplished musician; the medic who achieves fame by writing fiction. However much we may acknowledge the success in a limited sphere, we know that – if we were in that position – we would want a life that had other elements in it. Few, in the pursuit of success, would want to become labelled a "nerd" or an "anorak"!

Looking at a college group photograph, I wonder what they are all doing now. Each keen young undergraduate will have made his or her choices in life, careers will have come and gone, families have been brought up and flown the nest, battles with disease have been fought and won or lost. And looking at them I wonder what they would make of my life, if I were facing them now as an investigatory panel. This is the secular equivalent of the idea of appearing at the last day before the judgement of God. You need to give an account of yourself, perhaps before God, perhaps before your peers, but certainly before yourself. In *Hamlet*, Shakespeare has Polonius say "This above all: to thine own self be true ..." (I.iii.82), and that advice is both a challenge and a source of confusion. For we may indeed wish to be true to our own selves, but remain confused about who we really are. How can we be true to ourselves unless we know what we stand for?

A possible exception to the more narrowly defined measures of success is that offered by religion. Being told that you have an eternal soul, destined for higher things no matter what happens to you on earth, or that you are one of a chosen elite, offers a vision of a greater good or purpose that sets earthly suffering and failure in a wider perspective. No matter how harrowing life becomes, we know that all will be well in the end, because there is an as-yet-unrevealed purpose in all this. Clinging to a religious vision, the failure of almost everything else in life can be made bearable. Success is not of this world and, in times of trouble, religion can be a most effective opiate to dull the pain of reality, as Karl Marx pointed out. The problem is that the grand, universal goals, which were once the keystone of religion, and appeared to offer objective measures of quality and value, are now largely seen as human constructs. They become optional, and the religious route based on them therefore becomes just one aspect of life alongside others. We may choose to join a religion as we may choose to enrol in any other special-interest club. That is not to deny the value of religion's insights, but merely to observe that religion may be used (or misused, some would say) in a narrower context. Then there are secular alternatives to religious goals. We replace the life of holiness by increased standards of living, heaven by the prospect of a long and healthy retirement.

Yet, whether they are secular or religious, realistic or not, objective or human constructs, goals of some sort are essential to human motivation. But that raises a fundamental question: do I first seek to understand who I am and then shape my goals accordingly, or can I only understand who I am by looking at the goals that I have set myself? We start to stray here into the territory of existential philosophy, with its claim that existence comes before essence, and that we take responsibility for shaping and determining the person we are to become. Nothing, for an existentialist, is fixed beforehand; there is no absolute essence to which we should make our lives conform. We are free to choose our own measures of success, and – from the existentialist standpoint – the real success in the art of living stems from recognizing and responding to the fact that we are free to do the choosing.

But with so many competing values and goals to choose from, holding together the ones we have chosen to enable our individual life to make sense would seem to require skill, clear-sightedness and balance. And that may be summed up in a universally lauded quality: integrity. But integrity may not always be quite what it appears, as we shall examine in the next chapter.

4. The temptations of integrity

Ideals can be dangerous. The worlds of media and sport often encourage the cult of celebrity, where a successful person's image is carefully crafted and enhanced, presenting an ideal to which the humbler majority might aspire but know they will never achieve. The fact that not everyone can achieve the ideal, or that some will cause themselves harm in the attempt, or end up being exposed as a fraud when they pose as something they are not, does not mean that having an ideal is harmful in itself. We need to have ideals and set goals in order to give our lives direction. The problem is knowing how to relate the ideal to the actual. In this chapter, I shall argue that, for most people most of the time, life is something of a compromise, and pretending it to be otherwise is one of the most common delusions and hazards in the way of developing a realistic and positive sense of "me". Groucho Marx's famous line "I don't care to belong to any club that will have me as a member" is a classic expression of the mismatch between what one aspires to and what one is.

Of all the ideals to which the developing self can aspire, the one that commands the most universal respect is integrity. People of integrity are invulnerable to criticism, do not have to try to hide parts of their private lives from the public gaze, know exactly what they believe in and stick to it. They are incorruptible: honest through and through. Most of all, they can be trusted. When they act, they are sure of what they are doing. When they state their beliefs, they have no doubts. But are there really people like that?

I suggest that the above description matches fairly closely what many people understand by integrity. If your life is a mess of confusions, your relationships fragment and you are accused (rightly or wrongly) of deceit or insincerity, you long for a sense of certainty and solidity, a feeling of having done the right thing. Integrity becomes something to be craved, and therein lies its danger. For the desire to achieve integrity may bring temptations to create a damaging semblance of an integrated life.

Integrity involves following your own principles and values without fear or favour. At its best it offers a well-balanced view, free from petty, self-referential perspectives, guided by reason and conscience. But, of course, you can act with integrity and yet be wrong. For the rightness of action depends on three things: information, values and reason. If your information (from your own senses or that given by others) is wrong, then any decision you take on that basis will be distorted. You may order a pre-emptive strike against a nation, based on the assumption that it has weapons of mass destruction and is taking a hostile stance towards you, and yet retain your integrity (provided that your values permit killing in self-defence) once the evidence on which you took that decision is shown to be false. The standard requirement (as in most legal and business matters) is that you should have carried out due diligence in the assessment of the evidence you were given. Thus you lose your integrity if you suspend your critical faculty because a piece of evidence you are given is particularly welcome or unwelcome. Equally, those who hold different fundamental values will – while retaining their integrity – take very different positions. Thus the person who volunteers to fight and the conscientious objector may be equally true to their beliefs. And, of course, if you have genuinely tried to come to a logical conclusion about what to do, but have become muddled and reached a decision that is later shown to be foolish, that need not threaten your integrity, but only your intellectual abilities.

Plato sought the integrity of both the individual and the state, and saw both as exemplifying a tri-partite structure. Just as within the state some were most suited to labouring to produce the basic necessities, others to guarding and organizing the state, and the few philosophically minded to ruling the other two categories, so he believed that, within an individual, the basic appetites and spirited nature should be ruled by reason. Thus, on the Platonic scheme, integrity is possible once reason rules, and that balance within the individual generally holds true.

So the person of integrity is expected to take a principled view, mediated by reason. And if you want to bring someone down, just attack their integrity. Politicians do it all the time; to hear a debate between presidential candidates in the United States is to hear the harsh, scratching sound of knives attempting to get through gaps in the armour of integrity. To change one's mind may be the only reasonable thing to do in changing circumstances, but it is very difficult to resist the temptation to cover over such shifts in opinion, for fear of being thought of as either weak or acting to please, rather than of acting from conviction. Defending integrity remains paramount if you want votes. We are all similarly tempted to do whatever we can to maintain the sense of our own integrity, and to defend our reputation whenever it is challenged. And the danger of the protective stance towards our own integrity is that it morphs into a counterfeit form, presenting the semblance of sincere conviction without the substance. And that route, as we shall see, leads to fanaticism and fundamentalism: the craving for some ideal, theme, or cause to which we can give ourselves without reservation.

A person in search of a cause is a person hunting for counterfeit integrity. Those who genuinely find themselves committed and integrated in their lives, do so without even realizing what is happening. It's one of those cases where wanting something is a good indication that one is not going to achieve the genuine article. The clearest example of this is the desire to be famous, as opposed to the desire to do things as well as possible (as a result of which fame may or may not come). Those who crave fame rather than excellence are likely to achieve a form of fame that is far from excellent, and there are plenty of people who appear famous for being famous and little else; if you doubt this, just read Mark Rowlands's *Fame* (2008), in which he explores the phenomenon of a "new variant fame".

To explore the temptations of integrity, we can do no better than to start with the existentialist philosophers of the twentieth century. Heidegger himself was a rather problematic figure when it comes to integrity. He briefly but notoriously supported the Nazi party in the 1930s, and his personal relationships hardly stand close scrutiny, but we should not allow his personal life to colour the importance of his philosophy. There are two aspects of his work (to be found in his *Being and Time* [1927]), that are most relevant to our theme. The first has already been mentioned: that he saw us as thrown into life with a particular set of circumstances, and therefore forced to make our choices and decisions from that point of view. The second, and most instructive for thinking about integrity, is his view that we are all tempted to take up social masks.

In our day-to-day existence, we do not have time or emotional energy to deal with everyone we meet on a sincere and personal level. If we go into a shop we will (hopefully) treat the person at the checkout with respect and politeness; we may even offer some friendly word, about the weather, perhaps, or how crowded or empty the shop happens to be. But we are treating them essentially as a functionary. They are there to do a job: they are selling; we are buying. We therefore treat them as a vendor; they treat us as a customer. And that phenomenon of acting within roles extends throughout society. Doctors or solicitors deliberately look at the objective facts about those who come to consult them, maintaining their professional stance by detaching personal feelings and preferences. Without that detachment, the differentiation of functions within a complex society would be quite impossible. But Heidegger pointed out that we have a tendency to take this a step further, and to identify ourselves with the masks we use when dealing with one another. In other words, we deliberately bracket out those elements in ourselves that are not relevant to what we want to achieve in any encounter. We choose for ourselves an image of what we feel we want to be, and then act in role, not allowing the whole of ourselves to be engaged. And, of course, we may need to adopt a succession of such masks, each one appropriate for a different aspect of our life: kindly parent, music lover, concentration camp guard.

Now, to some extent, the adopting of different masks at different times is understandable and inevitable. Who'd want to share a bed with a merchant banker unless they were also a lover? Who'd want a head teacher as a mother? The problem occurs when one of those masks becomes so important that it swallows the others. The result is a counterfeit integrity: the person with a single, dominating mask is in danger of becoming a fanatic. At the innocent level one may become an "anorak" or "nerd"; at the dangerous level, a terrorist.

In religion, counterfeit integrity will not allow beliefs to be examined and questioned; those who do not conform are excluded and condemned. Throughout history, too many people have been shunned (or, sadly, killed) for failing to conform to beliefs, in the mistaken view that the "integrity" of a religious community can only be maintained by requiring everyone to conform. But those who condemn the non-conformist are trying to defend a *counterfeit* integrity. Examples of this counterfeit form of integrity include the witchfinder and the fire-and-brimstone preacher; both wear a mask that is brittle and impervious to reason, believing it to represent their own integrity, and a valid defence of their beliefs.

Heidegger pointed to the temptation of accepting a fixed role, rather than starting with the given situation into which one has been thrown. Accepting "integrity" on such terms is to live in an inauthentic way. For existentialists, integrity is about acknowledging your central role in shaping and taking responsibility for your life, rather than accepting a fixed persona offered by society.

Heidegger's existentialist philosophy, although hardly an easy read, is profound and well worth exploring in the quest for understanding "me", but for our purposes, it is enough to recognize the temptation of allowing a mask to become a counterfeit for a fully integrated self. A psychological approach to the same issue might explore how people adopt strategies for achieving what they want by following a particular pattern of behaviour. There are any number of roles that people can play, both dominant and subservient, some taken up unconsciously, some as a deliberate ploy: the person who is always playing helpless and in need; the fool in a classroom; the clown in the office. Masks or games involve adopting a view of "me" that attempts to exclude (or make subservient) all but the particular facets of myself that I choose to display.

Sartre introduced another concept that is relevant to our exploration of integrity: "bad faith". He argued that people can be tempted to do what is expected of them, rather than taking responsibility for their own actions and choices. Bad faith allows a person to blame others, or circumstances, for what happens, and for Sartre it is the very opposite of integrity. Faced with a difficult situation, the temptation is to act in bad faith rather than with integrity; it is a way of getting rid of responsibility for what seems too difficult or daunting. For Sartre, to act in good faith is not a temptation: it is a matter of seriousness and responsibility. Indeed, that tradition goes right back to Søren Kierkegaard, that troubled Danish philosopher of the nineteenth century, whose influence can be felt in the whole existentialist movement. He saw that what counted was the seriousness with which a choice was made, rather than the choice itself. And that seriousness was linked to integrity. For neither Kierkegaard nor Sartre is integrity the easy option, and many people prefer to take one of the escape routes into play-acting and counterfeit integrity. And that is understandable, because the easiest option by far is to accept the package deal. Society provides many opportunities to settle for a ready-organized "me". I can become the entrepreneur, the creative artist, the house person, the underdog, the activist, the martyr, the hero, the humble servant of all; but to take one of these as a conscious option involves setting aside my uniqueness in order to opt for something less.

It is difficult to overemphasize what a comfort and temptation it is to settle for the package. To find a community that will accept you unconditionally, that will give you a defined and settled role in life, that will provide you with a set of ideas and values by which to live, is a huge temptation, because it fulfils so much of what, as individuals, we crave. It has been a profound influence on the persistence of religion over the centuries. Whether religious beliefs are true or false counts for relatively little when compared with the sheer existential comfort that religion brings. Marx accused it of being the heart of a heartless world and the opium of the people. In many ways it is just that and proud of it, for it provides a sense of personal acceptance in an impersonal universe, a direction in a world that – as pointed out by Nietzsche – is drifting free of its moorings. To be "saved" is to be given recognition, a permanent value and meaning, and to know that, in an uncertain world, and whatever might happen to you, your life matters. Marx assumed that religion, once people gained more control over their own lives, would wither and die. How wrong he was. The power of religion is not diminished by intellectual attacks on the veracity of its belief systems; if that had been the case it would have disappeared long ago. Religion thrives in spite of its beliefs, because it offers the promise of a single cluster of ideas that outweighs all others: that you matter; that your life makes sense; that you are healed and saved; that – in effect – you are at last given the integrity for which you, in the confusions of your day-to-day life, have been longing; that you are a wanderer who has, at last, arrived home.

Religious packages seem to be the most effective and long-lasting, but there are many others: political movements, special interest groups, local community organizations, successful business networks, even the sexual freedoms of the early "lifestyle" or hippie movements of the 1960s. Buying into the package is tempting because it extricates us from the seriousness (the heaviness and lightness to use Kundera's terms) of facing life with only our own unaided efforts. Making and taking responsibility for your own decisions, and living with the consequences, is never going to be easy. Evaluating your own beliefs and, where necessary, changing your mind in the face of new evidence is also a struggle. It requires admitting that you may be wrong, that others may know better.

And hence it is within religion that there is the clearest illustration of the temptations of integrity. There are those who are sincere through and through, who give themselves wholeheartedly to the worldview that their religion teaches, who admit when they do not understand, acknowledge the limits of what we can know about the ultimate meaning and purpose of things, and yet feel positive in the direction they have freely chosen for their lives. They are the saints and the spiritual giants. But they only show up those who wish to appear sincere, to display their integrity, without that touch of authenticity. The latter are characterized, more often than not, by a ruthless inflexibility and defensiveness, a holier-than-thou attitude, and a sense (brought out best perhaps by Anthony Trollope or Jane Austen) of the cringe-making images of hypocrisy. That, perfectly expressed, is a counterfeit integrity and the acting out of a longing to be something other that what one is. The point we may overlook is that, more often than not, the hypocrite craves genuine integrity: it is the craving to "be" someone that leads to the caricature of the longed-for ideal. Austen's *Pride and Prejudice* gives the most delicious example of counterfeit integrity, poorly disguised, in the person of the clergyman Mr Collins: ever rehearsing what he will say to create the right effect, unaware of how much his guard is slipping. But you do not have to assume that counterfeit integrity is only seen in such extreme cases, for a trace of it is universal. I am unique, and yet in order to feel comfortable I will constantly look around and ask who I am meant to be. What kind of "me" will be acceptable? What kind of image should that "me" have? What constitutes success, what failure? These questions assume that there is an ideal to which you wish to conform, a true essence of yourself, which, once revealed and acted out, will enable you to live with integrity. But is that the case?

A key theme for Sartre, and also in the philosophy of his partner, Simone de Beauvoir, is that existence precedes essence. In other words, we shape the person we are through the decisions we make. We do not have a fixed, given self that needs to find its expression, but have the far more serious responsibility of continually working to give ourselves essence. I am what I have chosen to become. Integrity is thus the result of holding together the various choices and decisions that you make; it is seeing your life being shaped in a way that is consistent with your views and thoughts; it is recognizing the limited range of what you can do, in the passage between being thrown into life at birth and leaving it again at death. At one level, everything is contingent and may therefore be seen as futile, at another it is the greatest of challenges to make something meaningful of life in that brief time that is allowed to us.

For Beauvoir, we have moral obligation because we are able to think and thereby transcend ourselves. Decisions weigh heavily on us because, while the past is given and determines what happens in the present, the future always lies open, it is something we are able to shape, it is the location of our freedom. (Her major work dealing with this whole issue of decisions and choices is *The Ethics of Ambiguity*, written in 1947). The ambiguity is between the self that the past has made us, and the future possibilities we are free to take up, just as our bodies are a given fact and our consciousness transcends it. It is the freedom to go beyond what we are now that gives rise to freedom and morality, along with the sense of responsibility that comes with it. One is actually free all the time, but one is only morally free by an act of will. In other words, in moral terms one acknowledges freedom and is therefore able to take moral responsibility. But a key feature of her ethics is that moral values and choices are not simply those chosen by the individual; because all values are shared, they are social. To be a person is to be in relationship with others; only on that basis can morality make sense. So the development of the self cannot be a solitary matter; that development can only come about within a world of shared understandings and values.

But let us return to Heidegger for a moment. One element of his later philosophy is his idea of "enframing". He argued that, as we encounter the world, we see things in terms of what they do for us, how we may use them. This tree becomes a source of wood with which I can make something: it is "enframed" in a way that makes it useful. So let's explore the possibilities of this idea for a moment. In encountering the world, I enframe elements in my experience in order to make them relevant and manageable. The world is just too complex, too ambiguous, for me to handle. I need to get to grips with it, to set the parts of it that are relevant to me within a limited frame of my own making. When the mind of the baby goes hunting, it is looking for what can provide satisfaction. The breast is "enframed" as a source of nourishment and contentment; whether it is also a thing of beauty, or a source of sexual pleasure, is, for its purpose, irrelevant.

This concept of enframing can lead us to appreciate the difference between integrity itself and the temptations of integrity. Integrity is the description of a process: it is the description of what happens when someone routinely takes into account everything of which he or she is aware, and therefore takes a view that does not deliberately distort a decision for the sake of other, separated, aspects of his or her personality. Integrity happens when you are sincere:

without fault-lines or cracks in your decision-making process. But the temptations of integrity are those of wanting to appear to be of a piece when life is actually pulling in many directions: to get to grips with and "enframe" the self; to try to get hold of an image of ourselves that we can use. "This is the sort of person I am", I think, "and I present myself as useful to you on that basis". But inevitably, as soon as I think in that way, I will have enframed a limited and distorted version of myself.

There is also a political aspect to personal integrity. If – as Hobbes, Locke and Rousseau argued – society is based on a social contract between individuals, or between citizens and the ruler, then the individual has a responsibility to conform to what society requires. To act with complete freedom would require disregard for the freedoms of others and result in chaos. Social life is only possible because individuals are willing, for the common good, to curb their immediate desires. But does such political and social conformity imply a loss of personal integrity? Clearly, there are times when an individual is convinced that what society or the state is doing is profoundly wrong and therefore chooses to rebel, to maintain his or her integrity even at the cost of life itself. Martyrs of all sorts put their integrity ahead of social conformity.

On the other hand, one might argue that an integrity based only on following one's own immediate desires is hardly worthy of the name; more likely, it is a tyranny of the appetites over reason (and Plato had much to say about that). Hence, it might be argued that the rational acceptance of one's political and social responsibilities is, in itself, a valid form of personal integrity: an integrity in which the self is fully embedded in its social environment. And, after all, where do our individual desires come from, if not from society? Rousseau argued that, in the natural state, people are content; it is with the arrival of society that temptations are offered and goods desired. So there can be no escaping the effect of our social environment on our personal integrity. Even the radical, facing martyrdom rather than conform, is being loyal not just to himself or herself, but to the whole nexus of ideas and beliefs that underpin radicalism. To reject the norms of one group is to prioritize those of another.

Whether we follow a set of principles, or choose to be integrated into a pattern of life that society promotes, we are involved in making commitments. Those who are committed may become fixed, limited, blinkered perhaps. They may define themselves in a way that closes their lives off to other possibilities or to acknowledging elements in themselves of which they may feel ashamed or embarrassed. That's always going to be the problem with a commitment that requires the exclusion of conflicting views. On the other hand, the refusal to make commitments of any sort leads to a vague and rootless life, without sustainable values. It is destructive of relationships, since relationships depend on some degree of predictability. We love people because we know what they stand for, who they are, what they love and therefore how they will be expected to behave in any given situation. A person without commitments is a blank: unpredictable and at the same time unlovable. So commit we must, for even the decision to make no commitments is a commitment of a sort. We cannot escape from that process, and we cannot escape from the fact that commitments, even more than choices, are ways of measuring our integrity. A commitment may illustrate true integrity, or it may be just a way of expressing the craving for integrity – committing to this person, or this cause, right or wrong, come what may, may seem noble, but at a personal level it may also be tragic.

Fear stalks the existential world of choices and decisions. Choosing one thing excludes another, and we have little idea of the consequences. Think back to crucial moments in your own life: when you first decided which subjects to opt for at school or college, and thereby started to shape your career choice; when you first glimpsed the person with whom you were to embark on a disastrous relationship, or perhaps the person who was to be the future mother or father of your lovely family. What if you had chosen otherwise? How would your life now have been different? Of all the possible worlds you inhabit, this is the one that results from your choices. This is nowhere more succinctly stated than in the opening lines of the Buddha's *Dhammapada*: "What we are today comes from our thoughts of yesterday, and our present thoughts build our life of tomorrow: our life is the creation of our mind". Clearly, as the Buddha pointed out, all things change and many factors that shape our lives are beyond our control. It would therefore be naive to think that our decisions can totally condition the future, but they are a factor, and the only factor over which we have direct control. Hence their importance and their threat.

So, faced with uncertainty about our future, the results of our choices or the factors in our background that influence us, we all do it: we all bracket out what we cannot handle, leave it out of our frame, and settle for a limited image of "me" for the purposes of getting on with life. If we think about it at all, we hope that the "me" that we use has a measure of integrity – that it hangs together without too many internal conflicts – but we can never be one hundred per cent certain that there does not lurk within us some inclination, some potential, to do something quite "out of character".

The temptation is to take this process too far: to reduce the concept of "me" to such an extent that we achieve an appearance of integrity only by discarding all those human elements that do not seem to fit our chosen image. But you are not a fixed entity, but the ever-changing result of the process by which you have encountered and engaged with the world. Some people cruelly say that you get the face you deserve, and sometimes it is sadly true that a person's face reveals decades of adopting an habitual scowl, while another shows the wear and tear of habitual laughter. Its less true that you get the self you deserve, since much of what you are depends on all those external things (and other people, of course) that shape your passage through life. The self you get is the self that you recognize in your hopes and fears and also in those things you regret, or for which you are grateful.

It's never a complete view, of course: other people may see things in you that you do not even acknowledge to yourself. But it needs to be a working view, enough to enable you to know who you are and set about making choices. Sartre made the important distinction between "being for-itself" and "being in-itself". Physical objects that we encounter in the world exist for us in the "in itself" mode, and when we try to survey ourselves as physical objects – in other words, when we define ourselves in terms of who we are "out there", the sum of our physical commitments, our job, our political world, our physical body even – then we exist only in the same way that other physical objects exist. But as an acting, choosing, willing subject I encounter a world and affirm myself within it. Seen in that way I am being "for-itself". The problem, as we cut out of the frame aspects of ourselves in the attempt to create a sincere whole, without the embarrassing human anomalies, is that we increasingly come to see ourselves as "in-itself": as objects. And acting as an object, as a functionary, as a pretence of something that we are not, is exactly what Sartre called acting in bad faith, and Jane Austen pilloried in the character of Mr Collins.

But this process is seldom rational, and the elements of the self that are set aside are still likely to lurk in the unconscious, waiting to catch us out at just the moment when we feel that we understand ourselves fully. Clearly, although there is no scope to explore it here, one might start to look at the whole relationship between the conscious or unconscious mind, as it influences this sense of personal integrity, whether genuine or counterfeit. In *Civilisation and its Discontents* (1930), Freud suggested that the stricter and more repressive the moral ideals to which we aspire, the more likely we are to repress those elements in ourselves that recognize the demand as being unrealistic. If we repress what we find unacceptable, we are already on the road that leads to counterfeit integrity.

Predictably, this chapter has gleaned its philosophical thoughts mainly from the existentialists, since it is they who have explored the meaning of self, of authenticity and so on. But existentialism is no longer flavour of the philosophical month and the intensity with which it explored the issues of human will and choice, and the centrality it gave to the individual ego, has given way to other concerns. In 1970, in her book *Existentialism*, Mary Warnock suggested that the existentialist movement was collapsing into sociology and anthropology. In other words, there came a time when discussion about human existence shifted its focus from the inner experience to the outward manifestation. If I want to know what life is about, I can describe it; I do not have to unpack my experience of it.

And, in a way, the shift in emphasis away from the existential questions, which had started in the 1950s and was clearly evident in the 1970s, enabled the rise of other approaches to philosophy and culture, including postmodernism: the sense that the creative subject had given way to a range of images and symbols that were gathered from and belonged to society as a whole. Who I am is more a matter of where I am in the social and cultural scheme of things, and if I describe myself I cannot help but do it is terms that society has given me: in the images of the media, the common currency of thought and language.

Continental philosophy's view of the self moved from the smoke-filled cafes of Paris, to the wider cut-and-paste world of the media. The world moved on, never better illustrated than by the new possibilities offered by the internet. In cyberspace there is no need to agonize over your authenticity: you can recreate yourself at will and present any image you like! Well, perhaps you can; let's see.

5. Living in cyberspace

If only Plato had lived to witness the arrival of the internet, he would have realized that the twenty-first century has given an entirely new significance to a story he told in Book 2 of his *Republic*: the story of the Ring of Gyges. Gyges is a shepherd in the service of the king who, following a storm and earthquake where his flock is feeding, looks down into a chasm that has opened up in the ground, and sees there a bronze horse and within it the body of a man, wearing nothing but a ring. He takes the ring, puts it on and, by chance while at a meeting with his fellow shepherds, finds that by turning it he becomes invisible and then by turning it back becomes visible again. Arranging to go to the court as a messenger, he uses this new power of invisibility to seduce the queen (we are not told how this is achieved, but it would be intriguing to know the sexual attractiveness to be found in invisibility!) and, with her help, to kill the king and take the throne. Plato's point in recounting this story is to compare the just and the unjust person, supposing that there were two such rings and one were given to each. The fundamental question is this: would you retain your moral principles if you knew that you could take whatever you liked with impunity? Would you resist the temptation to use that power to enhance your own position? Are we kept moral only by fear of consequences?

At long last, we have found Gyges' ring again, not in a chasm, but in cyberspace. But the ring takes a new form now; it offers the power to become an avatar in the virtual world Second Life. But for those who have not yet fallen for this ultimate temptation to reinvent themselves, let me explain. In a virtual world you create for yourself an alter-ego, an avatar. Avatars in Hindu mythology are incarnations of the deities on earth, but these cyberspace avatars work the other way round: they are based on the earthly and aspire to be heavenly. Constructing your own avatar, you decide whether you would like to be male or female; you design your body, your figure, your hair colour, your eyes. You can make yourself attractive to the same or opposite sex, as the fancy takes you. You become whatever you would most like to be, shape up the image of your avatar with the help of a little software, and then go walking in a virtual world. The Second Life website claims that "The Second Life world is a place dedicated to your creativity" and points out that your avatar is "your persona in the virtual world" and that you should not worry if your avatar does not quite live up to what you would like to be, because "you can change your look at any time". It offers you a new, virtual start, socially and physically. It gives an opportunity to test out possibilities that we might want to apply to this, first life. And we can freely do so because, unlike this life, where we are stuck with the persona that nature, chance and experience seem to have given us, and where (since it is real and not virtual) we have to take responsibility for what we do, here in the virtual world we can simply log off. We turn the ring of Gyges and vanish from the virtual world.

But, provided we stay logged on, that's where it starts to get really interesting. The Second Life website suggests that:

> Second Life residents are eager to meet you and show you around.
>
> Within this vibrant society of people, it's easy to find people with similar interests to you. Once you meet people you like, you find it's easy to communicate and stay in touch ...
>
> In the Second Life world, there's something new around every corner.

So you enter the virtual world and meet other avatars. They too have been created to be whatever their earthly owners wanted. As you meet them (or ignore them, if you choose) you decide what you would like to do with them, what interests you might like to share. Second Life may be totally respectable and just like ordinary life except more creative, more open to the imagination, and offering more opportunities to test out all that you might like to be. But it does not take much imagination to realize that, while some of these virtual environments are used for serious games, emergency simulation exercises and the like, the biggest single potential for all this is in the sphere of the erotic. In the world of virtual porn, you can be and do whatever you like. You can test out your real desires, and be as outrageous as you wish. But at the end of the session, you can log off. You stride on a different, virtual world, being whoever you want to be, but with the power – like Gyges – to make yourself invisible at any moment. You (in the form of your avatar) can act with impunity; you never have to live with the consequences of anything you do. As in an internet "chat room", where fantasy meets fantasy and you can test out who you'd really like to be, it seems that anything is possible.

Virtual environments are just the latest, and most sophisticated, form of alternative worlds available to those who want to test out and explore who they are. The media have always provided opportunities to invent and reinvent oneself: to present an image to the world, to take advice on presentation, on how to appeal to an audience, on how to attract a personal following. Once you are a media person (or perhaps, more accurately, once you have a media personality) you can live and present yourself both physically and through the media, and it is up to you how those two presentations compare with one another. Is your company really as big as its website suggests? Does your personal page on your website tell the whole story? Do you have a following in cyberspace? If so, do they really know who they're following? A big question for any media person is: do you believe your own publicity? Is what you are perceived to be in your chosen media an accurate reflection of what you are in the flesh? Is there a genuine integrity between the real and the virtual "you"? We live in an era where autofiction has become not just an art form, but a way of life. We are now able to create and upload an image of ourselves, interact with other uploads, and live in a second, virtual life, freed from the personal circumstances and limitations of this one. Through the use of personal blogs, websites or Facebook, people put themselves in the most public of arenas and in a way that attempts to preserve, enhance or even recreate their personal "me". But the problem is that my friends can do the same.

Going for an interview for a new job, I am on my best behaviour. I dress in an appropriate manner, and do not turn up drunk. But my prospective employer need only check my Facebook – or, more significantly, the Facebook entries of my friends – to see another side of me. Partying of an extremely informal kind is now published for all to see; it is a private feature of life that is now public knowledge. Does that make the self more transparent? Which is the real "me": the Saturday night camera phone snap or the immaculately turned-out interviewee? And should the one be allowed to impact on the other? And can we prevent them from doing so?

Using the media to recreate yourself in the image of the "me" that you would like to be, enhanced and given cyber context and purpose, can give a wonderful sense of satisfaction. To use Heidegger's terminology, you present yourself already "enframed": gathered up and presented in a way that others will find useful.

Any self-image that I present in the media is going to be selective and partial; it will contain only those qualities that I choose to give it. But such controlled self-disclosure is not new. Augustine famously wrote his *Confessions* as a way of presenting his conversion to Christianity and therefore as a tool for promoting his beliefs. We glean what we can about the personality of the man by what he tells us or chooses not to tell us. Rousseau is another classic example. His *Confessions*, which, more than any other book (except possibly those of Sartre or Michel Foucault), reveal the most personal and sexual proclivities of a philosopher, is clearly a work of autofiction. In a string of personal and sexual revelations, he aims to present himself as an innocent abroad, one who finds himself corrupted by society, and whose peccadilloes are those of the child playing in an adult world, waiting – perhaps rather coyly, given his inclinations – to be spanked for his naughtiness. In his case, and I suspect in many, a confession of guilt is also in part a claim to a more fundamental innocence.

The art is to cover your nakedness with clothes that appear to reveal your nakedness: to exhibit your weaknesses in such a way that your strength is paraded. Autobiography may so easily become a deception when it is based on a fundamental self-deception. We select what we choose to regard as significant in our lives. Thus we create for ourselves a narrative for our lives, with character to fit. And we do the same for others too, seeing them not in their absolute uniqueness and individuality, but as types, categorized in order to understand how they should be treated. We are used to selecting and making a narrative in order to understand another person, but the autobiographer makes that task both easier and more difficult for us: easier because he or she is already suggesting what should be regarded as significant; more difficult because we are no longer in charge of shaping the narrative and thus our own assessment of that person and our view becomes clouded with their own presentation of material. Hence the value of autobiography as a means of disguise or a vehicle to preserve fundamental privacy. Yet that is never quite the case. If, for autobiography, the almost-right story is a decoy for the absolutely right story, that only mirrors our own degrees of self deception. At any one time, as I reflect on my past, choose to see myself in a particular way and select one or more personal or social roles to play, I am writing my personal narrative.

And as I move through life, I may adopt one narrative after another. Some people clearly change and reinvent themselves a number of times, others remain fairly static in their life views and roles, but none are ever fully free from the effects of change on their developing story. Hence my description of myself, even in the privacy of my most personal moments, is a form of autobiography that only approximates to, never reaches a point of, absolute truth. In the actual, physical world a good case can be made for saying that existence precedes essence, as Sartre claimed. In other words, it is the process of living that shapes who we are. Not so with web-selves or with the autobiography, for there the author can decide his or her essence in advance, and then spin a narrative to illustrate it.

In the real, physical world, the self is built up over decades, through relationships, career moves, experiences, culture and so on. We are thrown into a particular set of circumstances at our birth. We grow and learn within a culture, influenced by family, friends and society, and gradually develop the face that expresses who we have become. It is a process over which we have a fair measure of control, but not absolute control. I can opt to change my life, and am not short of people who will help me to do just that, but I cannot fundamentally change who I am; those factors that have shaped me from birth will be lurking somewhere beneath the surface of my new image, waiting to take me by surprise, to remind me of times past, to provoke that unexpected response, that pang of memory or regret, or to rekindle the long-smothered fire of an old ambition.

In the real world we are plastic, mouldable, to the degree that is permitted to us by all that surrounds us, and by the legacy we develop and carry with us as we move through life. To be suddenly thrown into an experience of utter freedom, where we can become exactly what we want to be, do exactly as we wish and know that we are never going to be caught out in the act by someone who has known us for years is truly daunting. But that is what virtual worlds can offer. We can be free, utterly free, to construct the ultimate "me", free of inhibitions from childhood or fear of consequences. As with a computer game, when we zap freely, kill without mercy and assert But that experience of freedom, contrasting with our "real" selves in this first world, serves to illustrate what a limited and slowly constructed thing our original "me" is.

The modern experience of entering a virtual world is not so different from the imaginary worlds into which people have always entered: the worlds of literature, or art, or religious mythology, or social ritual; worlds in which our ideal selves may be celebrated, our dreams re-enacted, our mundane existence set aside for a brief period.

Marx criticized religion on the grounds that it offered the prospect of compensation after death for the hardships suffered in this life, and thereby offered a substitute for the real thing, which he considered to be the improvement of living conditions here on earth. Religion, he believed, was an illusion from which people needed to shake themselves free. Coming from a rather different perspective, Freud took a similar view: that the illusion of religion is something for which the mature person had no need. Now, whether or not you agree with Marx's (or Freud's) criticism of religion, it is interesting to apply his argument to Second Life. Whoever you may be sitting in front of your computer screen, hand hovering over the mouse, you are only a click away from digitally displayed, creative environment. In that new world you stride out as your avatar, you dare to do what in this life you would never contemplate. You live again, take your chances again, and improve your self-image any time you like. In other words, you are offered digital heaven! You stride out in your heavenly world without revealing your mundane self. A new life on the internet might seem to serve the same displaced human longing for which Marx and Freud criticized religion. But it seems to me that – following the logic of Marx and Freud – there is a serious question to be asked of any image of the self that is deliberately crafted, whether for the internet, the autobiography or other media. Does it detract from the task of understanding and developing ourselves in this physical world?

My concern is that there can come a point at which the web-self becomes more real, more immediate than the physical self: that we start to believe in our own marketing hype, or the narrative of our constructed autobiography. But is that necessarily dishonest? After all, when asked who "we" are, we already start to describe the ideal: the self we would like others to perceive, not necessarily the self that they do perceive. Our avatar in Second Life may reflect the essence of who we are or who we would like to be. Who is to say that it is therefore any less real than the self that physical circumstances have pressed on us? Suppose, like Rousseau, we are actually innocents corrupted by society. If who we really are has been thwarted by our circumstances, what might we have been if only those circumstances had been different?

Virtual environments and serious games can be used as tools for playing with values and for acting out strategies. As such, they make visual what philosophy and ethics have always done, examining various "what if" scenarios. But problems arise with any blurring of the distinction between game and reality. Where players in an internet-based game start to contact one another by phone, the game becomes part of their real, physical life. The real and the virtual interact. A paedophile, grooming young people through internet chat rooms, is acting out a fantasy. Once the game moves into reality and physical contact is make with a vulnerable youngster, the two worlds move together with potentially devastating consequences. Violent games are merely that: games. But how does the exploration of sexuality or violence within the gaming world relate to reality? Does it encourage thoughts that are then played out in reality, or does it let off steam in a harmless way? The assumption here is that any potential "me" is capable of all the range of human activity and emotions. The virtual world appears to offer an innocent outlet but, as with Rousseau, one can never be sure whether innocence is genuine or a cunning disguise.

As a rather sad postscript to this discussion, while revising the text, I read in the newspaper that a couple had entered into a real-life divorce because one of their avatars was having an extramarital affair in Second Life. The real-life wife complained that she had done everything to make her avatar attractive to her husband's avatar, and yet he had strayed. For her, the husband's avatar had revealed what she interpreted as his real-life inclinations. Subsequently, the husband became engaged to the person with whose avatar he had had the affair, even though they had not met in person.

Games and sports may play a significant role in allowing us to discover who we are. Competitive sports are said to be "character building"; in other words, the whole idea of collaborating with others in a competitive environment (e.g. football or rugby) or competing against all others (e.g. athletics) is in itself a worthwhile experience. Kittens play at hunting and attacking one another, preparing themselves for a world in which those who hunt best survive. And for the human species, knowing how to cooperate in order to achieve a common goal gives evolutionary advantage. Games are therefore the way in which – in a controlled environment – we can test out and develop the "me" that we want and need to create.

The testing out of ourselves alongside other people is essential for understanding who we are. We develop what is most essential in human nature through cooperation and shared goals. The self exists primarily in relationships. We discover ourselves as we discover how we impact on others, what difference we make. Making no difference, isolated from other people, we shrink inwardly, become non-persons; it is a technique that brutal regimes know only too well. So whatever process it is by which we shape ourselves, it is not one of isolated speculation, but of engagement with the world. We will not discover the nature of "me" by examining neural activity, as though the individual were an isolated machine. We may use autofiction – internet-based or otherwise – to test out our relationships, but that testing process will only yield results if it is applied to ourselves in our ordinary physical lives.

There is a fundamental difference between being aware of myself, and of being identified. I do the former; others do the latter. In the ordinary course of things, there are a good number of external things that might identify me. I am recommended by my bank to make sure that nobody sees me as I key in my personal identification number at the cash dispenser. I fear for personal information about me getting into the wrong hands. I have already had one of my credit cards cloned and used illegally, without the card ever having left my possession. We are understandably afraid of what is now called "identity theft". But, of course, by now it is quite clear that there is no way in which my identity can be stolen by anyone. It is not my identity as such that is stolen, but those chosen points within my personal web of experience that I use to define myself: my name, my address, my credit card number, my driving licence. From the external point of view, these things, along with my physical body, identify me. By them, I can be distinguished from others, but that is not the same thing as saying that they define me. Telling one make of car from another is not the same as understanding how the internal combustion engine works, or knowing the journey it is making.

We need others to be able to identify us, but we also want to understand ourselves. In reality, we know that our lives are transient, random, dominated by chance, at the mercy of an infinite background of influences. That we exist at all seems wholly improbable; everything might have been so different; we are blown by the winds of chance, insignificant dust within the universe. But to look at ourselves like that is painful, revealing what Kundera referred to as the "lightness of being". So, to make life bearable, we construct our own fictions. Nothing has changed with the coming of the internet and Second Life except the vehicle and ease with which we can construct and share our chosen self-images. It is a deeply engrained feature of human life.

But how is it that we develop this sense of self that we need to express? How is our sense of "me" related to the life that we have led thus far, which others can identify and to which they can give my name? To start to answer these questions, let us review the argument so far.

However much we know that the brain is the physical location where our sensations and thoughts are to be found, we also know that – in terms of our own experience, and of whatever it means to be "me" – the self is not to be identified with neurons. Nor, however, does the self make much sense if separated from the body. Everything I am aware of, and every way I express myself, depends on having a body. So we moved on to a phenomenological exploration of what it means to be "me". We saw that the mind plays an active role in exploring and relating to its world: it takes, uses, shapes and creates. It is not simply a passive recipient of experience, but an agent. And we explored ways in which, as agents, we can evaluate and direct our lives, looking at the various goals that we set ourselves and judge our lives to be a success. From there we looked at the desire to be seen to have integrity – to have a life that makes sense, without being torn by ambiguity and conflicting goals – and the counterfeit forms of integrity that emerge as the ideal clashes with the actual. And from there, we have explored the ultimate temptation: to recreate ourselves in some form of autofiction, whether through the internet or other media. We want to be someone, and to present our life as making sense, as having a definite place and value in the universe.

But there remains a central and fundamental question. How is the sense of self developed within a physical organism? It can't just appear from nowhere. We know it grows and develops through life, but how is that stored in the brain? What is it that gives continuity to my life? How is it that I know I am the same person now that I was as a small child? What is the process by which we develop "me"? To this – the central feature of our enquiry – we must now turn.

6. Mapping one to one

If you want to get to know someone, a biography is more useful than a brain scan. Indeed, a biography is the attempt to understand someone as fully as possible, not just to trace out what they have done, but also to try to understand how they see the world and why. Imagine you are asked to write a biography of someone you don't know. How would you set about your research? In all probability you'd want to know where the person was born, into what family. You'd trace significant influences, people, places, events that impinged on your subject's life. The significance of each of these for your subject will vary. Some major events – a world war, for example – may actually affect your subject only peripherally; others, like the loss of a parent, will be profound. You gradually build up a picture of what your subject has done with his or her life, and of all the relationships and influences that have impinged on him or her along the way. In doing this, you are trying to get a rounded image of the person as they are now; you are trying to get under their skin. And you rightly assume that to do this you do not need to carry out an operation on their brain or to await a full analysis of neural activity. What you need to do, in order to understand how and why they are as they are, is to understand their history, but to do so in a particularly sensitive and empathetic way. You would, in effect, need to draw up a map of their lives: a map not just of their time and space, but one that showed the locations of personal meaning, significance and value.

This brings us to the key idea of this book: that personal identity – what it is to be "me" – is a process of creating and using a map, scaled 1:1. Yes, that is not a misprint. The map we construct is super-imposed by our minds, full scale, over the universe. It is a map that contains what the universe itself does not: value, meaning, signifi-cance. The process of mapping is carried out by the brain, and the experience of being "me" is the result of a constant process of refer-encing new experience against what we have experienced before, accessed by a process we call memory. This idea develops Kant's view that space, time and causality were imposed on our experience by our minds. And it is from this aspect of Kant's philosophy that there developed the strand of thought to which we have referred many times already in the book – a strand that runs through Schopenhauer, Nietzsche and the existentialists – that sees the human mind and will as taking a positive role in constructing our experienced world.

But, in order to appreciate this idea of a one-to-one map, let us return for a moment to the art of the biographer. By examining the physical circumstances of a person's life, along with what they have said or written, the biographer is attempting to fill in the points of value and significance on the subject's map. The good biography does not simply state that she was born in this particular place or time, but teases out the significance of that for the subject: to be born a Jew in Nazi Germany, or the daughter of a billionaire indus-trialist, or in the slums of any city in the developing world. This is to place the subject's birth not just at a physical location, but at a physical location with meaning. How close knit was their family? Whom did they meet in their "formative" (an important word for this process) years? The biographer teases out layer upon layer of this map as it has been laid down and modified over time; let us now consider the method of its construction.

Every sentient being survives by using its senses to negotiate its way through life: finding food, avoiding threats, securing a mate. To do this it has a single point of orientation, to which the senses refer. I see a world in front of me and sense myself located in my head, looking out, even though I know that behind my eyes there are only bony sockets and the soft folds of brain. That is the most fundamental sense of oneself as an experiencing subject: one has a viewpoint. From birth, a child starts to become aware of and relate to his or her environment. As we saw earlier, the mind goes hunting for what it needs; it is not merely a passive recipient of experience. And as it hunts and finds, it starts to build up a map of those things that have significance for it. Within the first few months of life, the child will come to explore a widening world in which some places, people and experiences will be welcomed and others will not. From birth we are aware of ourselves as experiencing subjects, and of the world as gradually taking shape around us. We know it is there, outside ourselves, and yet we also make it our own (and feel comfortable or uncomfortable within it) as it takes on significance and value for us. The newly born do not yet know that they have a world outside their physical bodies. They cry because they sense a lack, and their first bit of mapping is to find a point of nourishment and comfort. From that moment, they do not just cry because they feel empty: they cry because they want to be at the place where they feed. The breast is the first place to be located on the map.

That process of mapping continues through life. We gradually build up a three-dimensional map that is there before us the moment we open our eyes every morning, and through which we walk throughout our waking life. This place is my home, this is where I work; I associate this house with being welcomed, that with being made to feel uncomfortable; here is a person I love, here is someone I would rather avoid. In our personal world, space is far from homogeneous. The key features of the map, of course, are the value, meaning and significance that it plots out before us as we walk through it. Would I like grapefruit for breakfast? A tiny bit of neural activity takes place, memory kicks in and the prospect of having grapefruit is related to all my past experiences: the refreshing taste, the pain of squirting juice in my eye, the distinction in flavour between red, pink and yellow grapefruit. I do the computation and make my breakfast choice. It is memory that enables our map to locate what we like. Without memory we would look on every person as a stranger, every question about what we like would produce merely a blank stare. We only know what we like because we can remember liking it.

Quite apart from giving birth to memory, time has its own significance for our mapping process. Far from the impersonal measurement of change, which is what science knows by time, personal time is divided up into moments of significance (birthdays, Christmas, holidays, the time the company went bust, the moment my friend died) and the neutral time in between. We are mapped out by our special moments, as well as our special places and people; that, of course, is what every good biographer appreciates. Thinking back there are certain moments in my life that I shall never forget; they have left an indelible imprint on my map. There are also whole chunks of time that have vanished from my memory: years whose imprint is so faint that it hardly registers.

Sociologists have long explored this phenomenon of the non-homogeneity of space and time. In *The Sacred and the Profane* (1957), for example, Mircea Eliade explores it in terms of religion, speaking of sacred spaces and times, of the nature and function of myth and of the symbols that enable us to find meaning in an otherwise impersonal world. But we need to take this a step further, because the process that sociologists observe actually mirrors something internal to each individual, and intimately related to the way in which our brains function.

Gradually, overlay upon overlay, we build up a map that has the three dimensions of space, along with time and significance. And notice that the last of these is a genuinely new dimension on the map. Some events are still important for us now, even if they happened a long time ago. Their significance gives them a place on our personal map that would not be accurately reflected in terms of physical time and space. Our passage through life is one of map-making. Every thought we have, every experience, every new encounter is automatically located in our personal space. We relate it to what has gone before, to the infinite number of experiences that have shaped us. With each new experience our map is reshaped a little to accommodate its significance; some experiences hardly register, others cause our map to be radically redrawn.

We start to construct for ourselves a personal space, based on the point at which we are located. In that personal space will be friends, places we have lived, events, things we fear and those we long for. At any moment we can be aware of how far we are from each of them: thinking about family and friends, knowing the way to go home, remembering special moments in the past. All of these things serve to define us; all form part of our personal map. There will be times when we sense everything coming together to make this place or moment special for us. We may literally sense the warmth of acceptance and self-acceptance, a sense that there is nowhere else we would wish to be at this moment, no other time in which we would choose to live. Sometimes it may be no more than a fleeting idea, or hint at a belief, and our mind and heart responds with an instinctive "Yes!". And every refinement of our personal space – as we enter a new relationship, move house, start a new job, learn a new language – impacts on the "me" that we become. Every new experience or thought is related to our whole background terrain, like a new overlay on the existing map. Love, death, loss and success all serve to redefine the self: all shape the personal space of our experience. For some, a particular point on the map of their personal space comes to dominate all others. They become fixed in their views, adamant about maintaining their single point of security. Some fear to travel; others feel claustrophobic; some long to be something more in the future, others look to a period in the past when they were most happily themselves.

Have you ever felt utterly lost, and then suddenly felt the comfort of a familiar landmark? Or woken as a youngster, blurry-eyed, suddenly to remember that it is your birthday? Or, in a churchyard, come across a familiar name on a gravestone? At moments such as these we can almost feel the process of mapping; we sense points of significance being marked on our global map. "I lived here once", we say, as memory digs around to reveal personal coordinates long forgotten. But who am I in this process of mapping? Well, consider the situation from the standpoint of your hypothetical biographer. He or she will be seeing something of you in each of these points on your map. The more precisely the biographer reconstructs your map, the more accurately they will have understood you. And you, of course, are in the middle of all this. You are the experiencing subject, the point of perspective around which the map of your world fans out. If you can describe your "self" (as opposed to your physical body) you will be describing your map.

Daniel Dennett has argued (in *Consciousness Explained* [1991]) that the self is a fiction we use to make sense of the world. Just as physical bodies balance around a notional point that we call the centre of gravity, Dennett suggests that the self is a "narrative centre of gravity": it exists to give a single point of focus to the story of our experience. So the self is essential but not physical, something that the individual creates: "Each normal individual of the species makes a *self*. Out of its brain it spins a web of words and deeds, and, like the other creatures, it doesn't have to know what it's doing; it just does it" (1991: 416). The view I am arguing for here is similar to Dennett's, in that you are not a separate entity within your body. But whereas Dennett thinks in terms of the building of the self in terms of a narrative or a web, I prefer to use the idea of a map, in order to focus on the way in which we personalize the experience of "our" world as we encounter it out there in space and time. You, the perceiving subject, have character, sense yourself as "me" and are recognized by others, because of the whole web of things that have shaped your life. You are the feedback that your senses receive from your brain; you are the result of the interaction between brain and senses. That feedback turns raw sense data into something experienced by "me". And that feedback gives "me" a place in the centre of a map of "my" world. That is why we experience ourselves as being in the world looking round, not tucked up in the folds of our brain.

And at once it becomes clear why the self can neither be equated with the brain, nor exist independently of it. The brain operates the most flexible of databases, in which every new experience mediated to it via the senses is a query that is referred to everything else. Just as primitive creatures need to respond to their environment to find food, so the most sophisticated of all known objects, the human brain, carries out the most elaborate of processes. Every experience is nuanced. Everything we encounter is referenced to previous encounters. Different parts of the brain go into action simultaneously in the process of consciousness and thought. Neurobiology may reveal which parts deal with sight, which memory and so on, but it is the overall effect that is the clue to the emerging sense of "me": the gradual building of sets of personal references that determine both what we experience and how we respond to it. So we should not think of personal identity as a single thing, existing somewhere, either in our brains (if you're a materialist) or in some separate world of thought (if you're a dualist). The self is a combination of two systems, operating simultaneously. The one is the experiencing subject, exploring and gathering information about its world, responding to it and living within it. The other is the brain, which uses all this information to draw our personal map. We are not identified with neural activity, any more than this book is identified with individual bits of binary information that result from the pressing of keys on this keyboard. Your brain, fed by data from your senses, becomes a machine for making the world personal, and thus for creating your sense of "me".

Imagine yourself putting this book down and looking about you. As you do so, your senses are recording the scene and at the same time everything is being related to your internal map. You glance at a photograph; it reminds you of a person, an event, a place. And with that recognition, in the process called memory, comes a sense of value and meaning. And the same happens with everything you experience: everything is shot through with meaning and value – that is what makes you who you are; that is what the biographer will want to know about. That is mapping in real time, scaled 1:1 across your experienced, personal world. The continuity of this process explains the phenomenon of feeling at home or feeling lost. When we see around us tokens of what we know, we are comforted by their familiarity. When they are absent, we feel lost. A scene means nothing to us, until our friends step into view. Or perhaps the scene feels good and comforting just because we are anticipating that we will see our friend. Or it may feel good because it reminds us of other places we have enjoyed: the gentle folding of Devon hills, or the brassy sights and sounds of a New York street. For me, visiting Devon always brings back memories of childhood holidays. Stepping out in New York for the first time, I had a curious feeling of familiarity: I was walking through a Woody Allen film! So books, films and art also contribute to your personal map. The warmth of southern France suddenly becomes familiar as a Cezanne; the northern English city a Lowry; sunflowers or curled clouds burst at you through Van Gogh.

Many years ago I went to visit my daughter, who was spending a year teaching in Japan. I had never been to the Far East before, and found myself alone in the utterly unfamiliar surroundings of the railway station in Okayama city. I stood there, my hands touching my suitcase and my camera bag, the only points of familiarity, waiting. Then, from out of the crowd, I saw my daughter approaching. I was suddenly, overwhelmingly, at home. Because my daughter has a dominant place in my personal map, other places – in this case, places visited together in Japan – now also take on personal significance. And it happens all the time. A smell, a snatch of music, a particular colour, a feeling of warmth: each suddenly reminds us of other similar things, it triggers off our earlier response, and we appreciate and give significance to the present moment. Memory confers identity. This is nowhere better expressed than by Marcel Proust in the Preface to his *Á la recherche du temps perdu* (2003), where he writes that on awaking at night he is not sure where he is or who he is, but gradually remembers all the rooms in which he has slept, and so comes into full consciousness.

Whatever we encounter, or remember, or think about, is not simply experienced as it may be in itself, but always in terms of the significance it has for us. Heidegger spoke of things being encountered in ways that relate them to ourselves, as "ready to hand", as tools that we can use. Our senses may record in an impersonal way, but the brain automatically checks them against similar experiences in our past, relating them to other points of significance on our world-map. It may be the style of the house or room, or the folds of the land enclosing a village in protective embrace, but there are places where we smile and sense that we could comfortably settle. They have triggered points of significance on our map that may have been long forgotten. It is as if we are swimming in a sea of significance.

Show me a room that someone has designed for themselves, and I shall know something of their personality. Minimalist and spacious, or cosy and cluttered, gathered about an open fire, or designed to lead the eye through a window to a distant view, rooms reflect where we feel at home, and thus reflect points of comfort and security in our personal map. We settle into our favourite room and take in at a glance all the comfortable surroundings that affirm who we are.

Seen in this way, the self corresponds to what we know of the process of growth and learning: that we become more subtle in our discrimination once we have had previous experience of something similar. To see is to relate; there is no perception that is not immediately made "ours" by being referred to our database of experience.

Memory loss is loss of self, and that is the tragedy of Alzheimer's disease and other degenerative brain conditions. The sense of self leaks away, the connections are no longer made, the map starts to degenerate. Of course, the perceiving subject may sometimes be blissfully unaware that the connections are no longer being made. This person is encountered as pleasant, but the connections that say that this is a son or daughter may fail. The experiencing subject remains, but the mapping process that turns that subject into a person no longer works properly.

Degenerative brain disease gives the lie to the two most popular theories of self: that it is identified with brain activity or that it is quite separate from it. The person whose brain no longer functions properly is visibly diminished as a person. They are no longer what they were. One cannot therefore think that the mind, or self, is independent of the brain. On the other hand, the sense of a person being a genuine "me", is not simply dependent on their present neural functioning; they are also what they have been since the moment of their birth. When a brilliant mind, like that of Iris Murdoch, is brought down by disease, we see most clearly that the final state is not what that person really is; they are all that they have been, done, written. But, sadly in a way, their self cannot be removed entirely from its neural roots; if it could, disease would not touch it. Hence the advantage of thinking of "me" as the personal map that is constructed by my experience day by day, built up to provide me with a guide and a sense of value, shot through with the memories that allow me to feel at home in myself and the world. Objectively, it may be recognized as a personal history; subjectively, it may be experienced as "me".

But can I deliberately choose to change my map? Or, if everything I have experienced in the past is added to my map as time goes on, does it not gradually thicken around me like a cage? The logic of mapping would suggest that I can – indeed must – change my map as I move through life. Nothing remains static; new experience comes in all the time. What I make of today's experience will shape who I am tomorrow; what I made of yesterday's experience has shaped what I am today. Some things, perhaps those laid down in our early years, may never shift, even after therapy has brought them into consciousness. Others are open to be re-evaluated.

My experience of being me is unique, but I can only explain and appreciate my individuality with reference to my connections: what I have in common with others, or where I differ from them; how I relate to them and how they relate to me. To be deprived of connections, put in solitary confinement, is a form of torture and tends to produce a loss of any sense of self. I am deprived of myself as I am deprived of my connections. The strong hold out against such torture only because they remember who they were, what was important for them, and thus maintain their connections and identity through memory.

Although each map is unique, the terrain that is mapped is shared with others. Thus, as I live and walk within a world that now has my personal coordinates imposed on it, I find that others share those coordinates (indeed, they may *be* those coordinates). Mother and child share a chunk of one another's terrain. Those who live in the same place, or share a love of music, or work together share mapped terrain. Even if I can only describe "me" in terms of my map, there is nothing isolating or solipsistic about it. Mapping is in the real world and in real time; the process of making friends is discovering shared points of significance – revealing, sharing and developing our maps together. Perhaps this process of mapping may explain the love of art, music or fiction. In all these things what is expressed has a definite shape, form, nature. The music flows and comes to a conclusion, the work of art makes a statement, the novel (if conventional) has a plot with a beginning, a number of events or problems to be encountered, and a resolution of some sort, which explains and draws together the apparently chance events of earlier in the story. We may love such things because they display a controlled environment in which the self is shaped to make sense; the artist, musician and writer have done for their creation what we actually try to do for our own lives. It may also explain the popularity of researching family history: the longing to be placed within an ongoing historical tradition, to know who we are, where we have come from, and where we belong. And the place of our childhood has a special importance for us (whether its influence was benign or damaging), for that was where the map of our personal space was at its simplest, and where new points of significance shifted our life-map around most dramatically. But even before our birth, the personal space into which chance was to propel us was already gaining coordinates, of family, or culture and circumstances. To know exactly who we are now it would be necessary to see all that background, a task that Heidegger saw as impossible. To understand, we have to eliminate all but the most clear and central influences, just as a novelist needs to prune out much that is insignificant and inconsequential in order to provide a narrative that carries forward and makes sense. A plot, whether in fiction or in life, is a very selective thing.

In adolescence, young people need to push at the boundaries of authority by which their lives to that point have been circum-scribed, and parents and teachers become the most obvious targets. "What can I get away with?" is a way of exploring one's own ability to plan out a life. The coordinates of the teenage map enlarge with every act of defiance, whether or not it succeeds. It is curious also to note how quickly a deflated teenager can revert to the earlier comforts. Those just on the edge of adolescence may sometimes go back and visit their primary school, remembering the days of predictable safety when they were the oldest children in the school and that smaller world seemed safe for them. They want to show their former teacher that they have changed and grown. They also want to take a peep and make sure that the old, safe centre is still in place. Pushing the boundaries, or testing out new experiences, are conscious activities, but psychology has shown just how much of what we do is influenced by the unconscious. This does not invalidate our perception of the self as the product of a mapping process, but fits neatly into it. The earliest experiences are profound; they establish basic contours of the map. Later details are added, overlaying but not removing the deepest reference points of pleasure or pain. As we survey the conscious map we may see only the later details; the deepest contours of the emotions remain hidden until – through therapy or in dreams – they are revealed.

Indeed, the clearest experience of the mapping process happens when we dream. How often, in dreams, have we wandered through the landscape of an earlier time? I may find myself moving from a childhood home, turning a corner and finding myself in a later workplace, and thence into some other piece of terrain. Although confused and jumbled up, meeting quite the wrong people in the wrong places, dreams often evoke experiences through a sense of place. In one dream (details of which remain a matter of absolute confidence between my then therapist and myself), I found myself sitting on a naturist beach, wearing a clerical collar, which I was having desperate trouble trying to remove! That may reveal at least two different layers in my personal map, linked together by longing and trauma. Psychology has rightly identified dreams as a crucial way of engaging with the unconscious; dreams allow the deepest levels of our map to move up through the subsequent overlays and engage with present issues. In dreams, mapping anomalies are exposed and sorted, sets of coordinates set alongside one another. You wake after a dream and may, for a moment, be quite "disorientated" until your present map is established in consciousness and you are quite "yourself" again.

For those who are religious, their beliefs form a significant part of their map. Indeed, the practice of religion – whether in one of the Western traditions or the Eastern – is shot through with symbolism that helps people to locate themselves within a world of meaning. The layout of a church or temple, the actions of acknowledging an altar or an image, the sense of a community gathered to celebrate: all of these things are powerful within the overall map of significance in which we find ourselves. All tend to help us understand who we are by providing sets of beliefs and values that give us a personal location in an otherwise impersonal world. Of course, this sense of meaning and value to be found in the practice of religion gives religion a significance far greater than the beliefs within which it is expressed. To believe in an external deity existing somewhere within the universe, for example, not only goes against our scientific knowledge, but is totally inadequate as a religious concept, and (in terms of Christianity, Judaism and Islam) would be regarded as idolatry. Whatever "God" may mean, it can't mean that, although that does not appear to prevent many from claiming belief in such a god, and even some eminent scientists thinking it worthwhile to argue against it! But what might it mean to believe in the kind of god that the Apostle Paul is said to have proclaimed in Athens: one within whom "we live, move and have our being" (Acts 17:28)?

It might mean, of course, that "God" is the name some people choose to give for the most fundamental set of coordinates on their personal map: not a being within their world, but the whole world, seen as personal. Such a god is not part of the world revealed by science, but is nevertheless the most fundamental way of understanding the self and the world in personal terms. And the religious coordinates may give a most comforting sense of meaning and purpose. We are "at home" wherever we are, if our basic values and interpretations go with us in the form of a "God" who encloses the whole of our map. For those who might want to complain that this view suggests that God does not "exist", or that he is merely a human construct, I would reply that you and I are also human constructs. If we are trying to understand what it is to be an individual, then I'm sorry to tell you that in purely physical terms you do not exist either. There is no point in that skull of yours where you will find something that is you; all you will see is the most complex of neural processes, busy mapping out significance and meaning onto the constant stream of experience. To take a very different example, within the Tibetan Buddhist tradition, as part of a visualization practice, a person imagines that they have become the Bodhisattva (a Buddha being) that they have conjured up in their mind's eye. They therefore look on the world as though with eyes that are already enlightened. The values represented by the image are taken into the meditator's own personal map of significance. The religious aspects of this awareness of self is far beyond the scope of this book, but if the theory of the self as the process of mapping one to one is correct, then it gives religion, and even the concept of "God" an interesting, important role that is compatible with science, and utterly incompatible with literal, fundamentalist beliefs of a quasi-magical and unscientific kind.

The principle of mapping may be explored in many contexts, but perhaps the most instructive for understanding "me" is to consider it as a way of exploring relationships. The longing for love is the longing to find someone whose map has key points of value that match, or complement, one's own. To be among people whose maps are radically different is to be challenged, perhaps negatively, if our values are suddenly threatened, or positively, as when travel is said to broaden the mind. But seeking a friend is seeking someone who will become a significant part of one's own map, and for whom one will become a significant part of theirs. As we share our mapped terrain with other people, we create together a personalized world.

The map is, of course, no more than an analogy for the process of becoming a person, and like all analogies it has its limitations. In its literal form, we tend to see the map as one thing, the person drawing it as another, and separate from both of them is the terrain that is being mapped and which now gets represented on the piece of paper before us. The process of developing as a person, and of personalizing the experienced world, is far more subtle. The map is not separate from the world; it is not a paper representation of our homeland, tucked somewhere behind our cerebral cortex waiting to be consulted! The map really is scaled 1:1: out there, like an overlay on the world described by physics. It is the world of meaning and value through which we move and which we construct and share with others.

The analogy of the map is also stretched by the idea of "me", for the self is both the map (when it is being described – by myself or by others), the centre of consciousness that does the mapping (when it is the experiencing "I") and the feedback that the senses receive (when the self evaluates, chooses, plots its way). The difficulty with this is that, in our ordinary day-to-day existence, the acts of perceiving something with the senses and mapping its significance for us happen simultaneously. We don't first register a red object and then later, after consulting our memory and map, conclude that it's an apple and that we enjoy eating such things; both things happen simultaneously. The "I" that experiences is constantly flooded with the "me" of interpretation and self-awareness. Self-awareness – the very essence of being "me" – is, of course, a mental phenomenon, but it has a physical basis, and that basis is the recording and mapping function of the brain, combined with the interactive relationship between brain and senses. We cannot see the neurons firing, but we can – as it were – stand beyond and above the processing and mapping functions. Call it sensitivity, call it self-transcendence, call it enlightenment (religious or otherwise): it is the ability to see ourselves other than through our own eyes. It may be possible to do that in isolation, but it is far easier to do it with the help of other people, where it is one of the great benefits conferred by friendship.

But our process of interactive mapping cannot go on for ever. There will come a point when we have to face the ending of life. For many thinkers, the prospect of death hangs over us, bringing into question the significance of everything we do. So it is to this that we must now turn.

7. Letting go

Euphemisms sometimes give words a bad name. The expression "letting go", which once had the simple meaning of releasing one's grip on something, allowing it to be free of one's control, has now come to be a euphemism for dismissal. Companies "let people go" when previously they would have "given them the sack", "laid them off", or simply "booted them out". But those other expressions are more accurate, since they indicate a positive dismissal. Strictly speaking, "letting go" should only happen when an employee wishes to go, and the company allows him or her to do so. So, in this chapter, we shall consider "letting go" in its original, positive sense: the releasing of our grip to allow what we have previously held to be free from our control.

So far we have explored the process by which our identity is built up through adding points of significance to the personal map that we superimpose on our world. That process is cumulative – from the first simple discoveries of the new-born, to the elaborate network of interests, relationships, values and emotional entanglements that build up as we grow older. But even if we become fearful misers, hoarding everything we can get our hands on, sooner or later we are going to have to face the fact that things will slip from our grasp. In the trajectory from birth to death, life involves as much letting go as picking up.

Buddhist philosophy teaches that the root cause of human dissatisfaction with life is the tendency to crave and grasp. This is not simply a moralistic plea for a simpler lifestyle, but is fundamental to the Buddhist understanding of the nature of reality. The Buddha observed that everything in this world is in a state of change, and that nothing has a fixed essence. Hence, the attempt to cling to something in the hope that it will offer permanent satisfaction is ultimately self-defeating. If we crave for that which is impossible, we will be frustrated; if we want things to be perfect and permanent for us, we will be dissatisfied. That view is not distinctively Eastern, for it was also put forward in ancient Greece by the Stoics. And the personal response to that view – for both Buddhists and Stoics – was one of accepting, even welcoming, the sense of letting go and of enjoying what life provides without hoarding goods or craving status or fame. The Buddha is recorded as saying "Because of greed for wealth the fool destroys himself as if he were his own enemy" (*Dhammapada*, 355) and Marcus Aurelius, in his *Meditations*, offers the following thoughts on transience and fame, made more remarkable by coming from a Roman emperor:

> This mortal life is a little thing, lived in a little corner of the earth; and little, too, is the longest fame to come – dependent as it is on a succession of fast-perishing little men who have no knowledge even of their own selves, much less of one long dead and gone. (Book 3, §10)

This has both philosophical and personal implications. Philosophically, it is the recognition that concepts and ideas give rise to ideals and a sense of perfection, whereas reality is always a matter of limitation and compromise. Personally, it is a recognition that we are naive in expecting to find perfection and permanence, whether in relationships, the goods we acquire or those things that appear to give our lives meaning, such as work or status.

Letting go is not optional. Whether the universe will continue to move outwards towards a future of absolute cold, with all its energy spent, or whether it will one day start to implode again, ending in a Big Crunch in perfect symmetry with the Big Bang with which it started, is a matter for physicists to predict. What we do know is that – one way or another – the sum total of this world is zero. Whether or not scientists at CERN discover the elusive Higgs boson, we know that matter has formed in some way from pure energy, has cooled and crystallized, differentiating into the elements of which this whole, huge, elaborate world of ours is made up. And yet, however wonderful and seemingly inevitable the process by which our world has evolved, we know that nothing in it lasts for ever. "Dust thou art and unto dust shalt thou return" may be the traditional thing to say at a funeral, but it carries a universal and inescapable truth. So the art of living, and of understanding and cultivating this "me" that is my identity, needs to explore how we set about letting things go. And, if the Buddha was right, that process should lead to contentment rather than despair.

But notice here a fundamental divergence between Buddhist philosophy on the one hand and the Western, existential tradition on the other. In the writings of Albert Camus, for example, there is a contrast between what we wish life to be and what it actually is. Life is fundamentally absurd, and to struggle on even when we know that nothing can be achieved only serves to highlight that sense of absurdity. The temptation to find an overall explanation and purpose, as opposed to accepting the given facts of life, is illustrated by the different reactions of priest and doctor in Camus's novel *The Plague*. The priest tries to understand sickness either as punishment or test, while the world-weary doctor struggles on to deal with the plague. To develop a brilliant writing career and then die young in a car crash, as Camus did, only emphasizes the absurdity of life.

But to say that something is absurd suggests that it might have been reasonable but is not. Absurdity is an affront to reason. So if we are led to say that the world is absurd, it would suggest to me that the very notion of meaning and absurdity are wrong. If I complain that the rest of the universe is out of step with me, it is more likely that I am out of step with the rest of the universe. So let us turn the existentialists' argument on its head. Rather than saying that life is fundamentally absurd, because the random and transient nature of everything goes against our sense of meaning and purpose, we may need to revisit what we think of as meaning and purpose in a transient universe.

The parallel to building up our personal map is the letting go of those things that remain on our map, but over which we do not feel the need to retain control: which can be careers, people (particularly children) or possessions. Clinging on to growing offspring, wishing they were small and biddable again, is not only a source of personal grief, but is fundamentally destructive of any relationship with them. "Love and let go" was, and remains, good advice. But that is not simply because it is comforting, but because it matches reality; the failure to let go is a failure to understand that everything is transient, and that everything changes. Given the nature of the universe, that which does not change is already dead. And that which is already dead is even now disintegrating into the basic components and energy from which it was constructed in the first place.

But let's get more specific about letting go. At my age, I have already retired from more things than I now intend taking up. At one moment I complain that my computer in-box is clogged with inter-company mail, the next moment I log on first thing in the morning to find only two e-mails, one offering to rent me a country cottage and the other trying to sell me Viagra at discount rates! Suddenly I find that I am no longer at the centre of things: that the world (or at least the company) moves on quite well without me. Am I thereby diminished? Clearly, the sense that I have of "me" needs to take into account, but not cling to, things that are now in the past. If the tension between the ideal career and my actual career are not resolved while I am still working (in other words, if I do not get a balanced view of my work and its place within the overall scheme of things), then retirement becomes a problem, because I still hanker after the recognition that comes from being part of a workforce. Letting go in retirement requires letting go much earlier: the letting go of a fixed idea of what my working life is for. If I allow work to define who I am, it is hardly surprising that my life will feel empty once work is a thing of the past. Equally, if my life is defined by my role as parent and homemaker, then the experience of children leaving home and making their own way in the world will be a threat to me. Letting go enables me to be content to see my work being continued by others; letting go enables the young to be free to discover their own life safe in the knowledge that they can maintain a relationship with parents who will love them as adults, not attempt to encourage them to regress into childhood. But the ultimate challenge of letting go comes with the awareness that one day we will die. One day we will have to let go completely and see the world moving on without us. What does that do to the sense of "me"? Is it possible to be content to see "me" as a phenomenon of the past rather than of the present or the future?

Obituaries are curiously comforting things. Like a traditional murder-mystery story, you know there will be a beginning, a middle and an end, and that significant clues and pointers will be placed at strategic points. What has this person become? Their "self" – the "me" that they thought about when others described them – is fixed by death. As we have seen, until then life is plastic; it can be moulded. At death that plasticity ceases and we have to accept, as we approach it, that there is nothing more we can do to give significance to our lives. Preparing for death is not a popular thing to do; not since the middle ages, anyway. And do we need to do so at all? Wittgenstein rightly declared that "death is not an event in life. We do not live to experience death" ([1921] 2001: 6.4311), echoing the ancient Greek philosopher Parmenides, who dismissed death as a mere nothing. Life and death are incompatible; there is no point at which we have to experience our own death. So it is not death itself that is a problem for us, but its anticipation. Preparing for death is therefore a matter of seeing your life as a whole – as a rounded and completed thing – rather than something that, at any moment in the future, will be transformed into something better. It is the ability to say "This is who I have been" rather than relying on "This is who I want to become".

We may safely assume that, below the level at which some form of reflexive self-consciousness comes into play, the animal world is unaware of its own death. Animals and birds can fret and grieve over the death of their families and mates, but we may assume that they do not suffer from existential doubt about the meaning of their transient lives. At a lower level, there are remarkable films of insects continuing to feed while they themselves are being eaten, apparently unaware or unconcerned that they are about to die. But once we are aware of the fact of death, it colours our understanding of life. This is a key feature of existentialist philosophy. Heidegger was particularly concerned with death. We are living towards death: that is the direction in which we are heading. It marks the finite nature of our life. He claimed that the essence of human being [*Dasein*] lies in its existence, and that existence is a matter of engaging with the world, living the authentic life by distinguishing yourself from the mass of the humanity and the rest of the world that lies around you. Authenticity in existence is a matter of fulfilling your own potential. But we are always anxious, and that anxiety does not generally come from a specific threat, but from something far more general: a sense of our own finitude, of the fact that we are born and that we will die. Coming to terms with death as an inevitable fact of life is absolutely necessary if we are to achieve some kind of authentic existence. And, on a very positive note, Heidegger regards the acceptance of death as giving a sense of freedom, and of liberating the individual from the petty concerns that fill everyday life. The whole process of self-understanding, for Heidegger, involves the three different aspects of human existence: past, present and future. We are thrown into life, into a set of circumstances that tend to define who we are. But equally we transcend that past and its conditioning by looking to the future in order to give expression to our desires and aspirations. Hence the present moment is one of anxiety, sandwiched between the other two. We do not just exist: we exist in a context, with our past and our future. A human being is, for him, *Dasein*, "being there", set in a context that is always bounded by death.

"You haven't changed a bit!" is the ultimate compliment to those whose faces are lined and whose hair (if still present) is grey. It is also the ultimate lie. We love to think that we can remain fixed at some ideal point: that physical existence, beyond the ideal bloom of youth, is not really what we actually know it to be – a slow (hopefully) downhill path. But for the young the threat operates in reverse. To say to a teenager that they haven't changed since they were in primary school is an insult. They want to develop: want to get to what they see as their ideal age. To those whose lives appear to be an endless open future of possibilities, moving forwards is not just a challenge but a welcome adventure. Whether they will ever come to the point when they can say "Now life is as perfect as it will ever be" will depend on circumstances and their taste for verbal hyperbole! Most will suddenly find, along the path of work, families and mortgages, that the slope has flattened out and may even start to tilt downhill. Hence the fear of those birthdays – thirtieth, fortieth, fiftieth – that mark our middle years; they force us to acknowledge that we may have gone beyond that point in our lives when our powers were at their height.

Change and our limited lifespan is the true context of all self-awareness. If it were not so there would be no sense of personal value or tragedy, for everything, over an infinite amount of time, could be equally good or insignificant. Significance is only given because time is limited. But the fact of death also seems to cut across any sense of natural justice. Why is the world so unfair when it comes to the length and quality of life that it allocates to individuals? The mind that plans and sees meaning and purpose finds itself confronted time and again with the brute fact of transience. Random events shatter our plans, making nonsense of the apparent predictability of our lives. We struggle to be ourselves and mean something in the face of the random chances that befall any complex being in an impersonal universe. That is the theme of writers such as Camus or Kundera. If life has value, it must lie in the process of living, not in its end product, for its end product is death and the dispersal of the elements that have made up this complex, sentient being.

I have been revising this chapter on the eleventh day of the eleventh month, ninety years after the end of the First World War, and I am haunted by thoughts of the carnage. In particular, on the very last day of war, after the armistice had been signed, with only a matter of hours to go before the agreed time for the cessation of hostilities, thousands of men were still being sent forward to fight and die. Their killing and their dying could make absolutely no difference to the outcome of the war. What must have been in their minds (or that of their commanders) at that moment? To die for a cause, or even from natural causes, is one thing; to die because of an absurd whim, to achieve nothing, is quite different. It is the human imposition of absurdity on the natural order. But more chilling still, I feel, are photographs of people going about their business in the years immediately before the war, unaware of the senseless brutality that would shortly cut off their dreams of the future.

Death from natural causes is easier to square with an overall, rational view of life. In his *Meditations*, Marcus Aurelius says of death:

Death, like birth, is one of Nature's secrets; the same elements that have been combined are then dispersed. Nothing about it need give cause for shame. For beings endowed with mind it is no anomaly, nor in any way inconsistent with the plan of their creation.

(Book 4, § 5)

That allows for a rational "letting go", in contrast to the brutality of having life pointlessly taken away by a bullet in the last moments of a conflict.

In dealing with the chances that cut across our sense of weight in life, Kundera takes as his starting point Nietzsche's idea of "The Eternal Recurrence"; namely, that the *Übermensch*, or "supermen", are able to accept life exactly as it is, to the extent of being able to will that this same life should recur over and over again to infinity. That is a radical acceptance of the chances and randomness of life. It is accepting what is, rather than constantly looking for an ideal that is never actual; it is looking to this life, transient though it is, rather than seeking an alternative in heaven. But this is always presented as a challenge, rather than an easy option. Acceptance of things as they are is fine, generally, only when life is going well. Bertrand Russell describes death in terms of a river flowing more slowly as it reaches its mouth and finally flowing out into the sea: ideally, of course, because not all lives end in peaceful acceptance of a return to the universal. Sensitivity to the traumas that beset most people most of the time rather inclines the mind to rebel against such random misery. Yet for many, the idea that life ends in extinction seems to evacuate it of meaning and value. Perhaps that is why ideas about life beyond death are so popular and find an expression in such a wide variety of religious beliefs. Pretending that we can still be open to a future – that no line will be drawn, and that we will have a chance to make good for whatever we have done against our own better judgement – is a most comforting thought. On the other hand, to those brought up to fear judgement after death, the idea of extinction at death might seem equally comforting, for there is no sudden requirement to stand up and be counted.

Views of the possibility of life beyond death relate closely to the different ideas about the relationship of mind and body that we considered in Chapter 1. For the dualist, there remains the possibility that the mind – since it is utterly distinct from the body – might survive the latter's death. The literature on this is extensive, but those arguing for a disembodied existence post-death need to face the problem of personal identity. In this life we express ourselves and know others through our bodies (which includes, of course, our language and literature, since that requires movements of tongue or hand). It also requires a sense of time, because actions and words exist only within time. A disembodied existence seems to lack any means of identifying itself or communicating. It is difficult to imagine a disembodied "me". The other possibility, for those who hold a dualist view, is reincarnation: the view, developed particularly within the Indian philosophical and cultural tradition, that the soul or mind can inhabit a succession of bodies. The advantage of this view is that the self, in gaining a new body after death, has a means of expressing itself. But who am I if I have already inhabited an infinite number of bodies in the past and am bound to inhabit an infinite number in the future? Also, although it is not a logical argument against it, reincarnation seems to me to detract from the significance of life in this world here and now, if our present incarnation is merely a brief paragraph in a very thick book of my life. Such a view would, from a Marxist perspective, discourage an emphasis on improving one's situation here and now, on the grounds that (through the doctrine of *karma*, which, put simply, teaches that actions in this life determine one's next incarnation) one is at least partly to blame for one's present circumstances, and will, by moral actions, determine the soul's future destiny. On the other hand, from a materialist point of view, brain death automatically ends the existence of "me". This, of course, is logical and has science on its side. All that we have said about the building up of a sense of self, from the moment of birth onwards, requires the operation of sense organs and a brain. However much we may experience ourselves as other than our bodies, that act of experiencing is dependent on the physical body.

If, as has been argued here, we are essentially a dynamic process of mapping, using senses and brain, there seems no prospect of life beyond the point of physical death. Does that imply that death renders life valueless and pointless? It seems to me that purpose and value do not inhere in things, but in the relationship we have with them. I say something has value because I see the part it plays in life. In ascribing value, the key points on most of our maps will be occupied by other people. Similarly, other people, in their process of mapping, may hold me to be of value. We have already explored the idea of relationship being a matter of interlocking maps: I am a point on the map of a large number of people. For some, I might loom large (whether positively or negatively, I leave them to judge!), for others I am almost insignificant, or may have faded from view. And just as the death of someone of significance to me will not remove them from my map – they will still be there, accessible to memory, influencing my views, perhaps being experienced in terms of painful loss – so my own death will not erase my imprint on the maps of others.

The Buddhist view is that we are constantly changing as we interact with an ever-changing world. Unlike the Hindu idea of reincarnation, there is no separate self or soul to move on into another life, but the process of change (or "re-becoming", as the teaching is generally translated) is thought to continue through death and beyond. What I am now will influence the world of tomorrow, even if I am no longer alive. That teaching can translate into our language of mapping. What I call "me" is a feature that appears on the maps of all who have encountered me. When my senses and brain fail, "I" – as an experiencing subject – will no longer exist. But the significance of "me" will continue in the network of those whose maps have touched mine. And they, in turn, will touch others, and so on in a theoretically infinite, outwardly moving wave of significance. In the impersonal physical world, I shall no more exist after death than I did before birth. In the world of meaning and significance, while the human process of mapping and valuing continues, I shall have played a part, albeit an infinitely small one. That is a view to which both the Buddha and Marcus Aurelius might have subscribed.

There is another aspect of the self and death that raises serious moral problems. Letting go of aspects of the self in favour of others, or of a cause, is generally regarded as laudable. After all, selfishness is self-defeating in the face of death. Hence, those who die fighting for their country, of going to the rescue of someone in distress, or in any act of heroism, are celebrated for their selflessness. Their principles take precedence over their natural sense of self-protection. But what is really worth dying for? How do we decide? We have already explored ways in which people seek to give overall meaning to their lives. One of these is to identify with a cause or an idea, but leads to the danger of counterfeit integrity. What, then, do we say of the suicide bomber? He or she has committed themselves absolutely to a cause to the point of volunteering to give their life for it. Now, it is often claimed that all such suicide bombers are brainwashed into taking part in martyrdom missions. And the assumption behind such a claim is that nobody who is rationally in charge of their life would wish to throw it away in a savage and life-destroying act. But that remains an assumption, rather than an observation. If an aid worker loses his or her life in a hopeless attempt to do good, one does not normally accuse the aid agency of brainwashing. It is seen as the ultimate act of self sacrifice. Hence we need to accept that, whether the act is seen as negative or positive, it is a feature of the letting go of life that people are sometimes prepared to die for a cause. And, in doing so, they surely sense what we have outlined above in terms of the interlocking web of maps: that their life finds its place and significance, beyond their individual death, in the cause for which they are prepared to let it go.

Some things are judged more important than the length of life. The French philosopher Michel Foucault, in order to affirm his chosen lifestyle, defiantly following the tradition of the Cynics of ancient Greece, deliberately risked fatal infection for the sake of being authentic, against the advice of many friends, and became the first well-known philosopher to die of AIDS. The cause for which he was prepared to die was – as he saw it – being true to himself and his sexuality. And there are other philosophers who have been described as facing death with calm equanimity: Socrates, Seneca, Epicurus, Hume. To them, the inevitability and naturalness of death was to be accepted as part of life, a final letting go. In his dialogue *Phaedo*, Plato even puts into the mouth of Socrates the view that true philosophers make dying their profession. To face death with equanimity seems to be the ultimate "philosophical" stance.

8. The illusion of "me"

Let's take the simplest example. You dip a stick into water and it appears to bend. That is an illusion, but it is one that you can work with. You can manipulate something beneath the water with the stick, guided entirely by what you see. You can put two sticks in the water and touch them together very precisely. For all practical purposes, the fact that what you see is an illusion makes no difference. You know that what you are experiencing is not how the stick actually is; you know it is straight, but that does not detract from what you can do with the stick. The implication of much of what we have examined so far in this book is that my sense of being a distinct entity called "me" is an illusion. But I want to argue that, just like the bent stick, it is a perfectly useful illusion. Indeed, in terms of being aware of our world, orientating ourselves and relating to other people, it is an absolutely necessary illusion.

However, describing the self as an illusion is counter-intuitive. If I say, "You are an illusion", you know it's not true. You know that, because you know that you exist. If you are polite and philosophical (and the two tendencies need not be mutually exclusive) you may not automatically dismiss my claim, but will consider what it is that I mean by "illusion" and how it might be applied to the self. So let's do just that. Stand back a moment and contemplate the subjective and objective aspects of the self. From the subjective point of view, what you know at any moment is the range of experience that comes to you though your senses: you look out into a world, you see, hear, smell, touch and taste it. And as you do so, you are conscious of yourself as an evaluator of experience; you are positioned at the centre of your experienced world. This wine tastes good: yes, please, continue to pour! I've been caught by those brambles before: I had better wear gloves. There is a constant flow of experience, evaluation and response. It is a process that you sense as going on somewhere behind your eyes, and as a monologue – in a voice that is clearly human, but not exactly your own – issuing from within your head, but heard only by yourself. But your centre of consciousness does not exist in a physical location. Behind your eyes there is no cinema of experience with a "you" sitting there watching. There is no vocalized monologue. There are just the soft, grey folds of brain within your skull. You know the brain is working, rather like the regular whirring of the hard drive of a computer, and it's consuming a fair amount of the energy that you need to ingest each day in order to function, but there is no single point that is you: no image on a screen; no computer printout. We know that being a living, sentient being depends on the activity that goes on within the brain, but there is nothing physical to be found that corresponds exclusively to the subjective experience of selfhood.

But consider "me" from an objective point of view: from that of a biographer, if you like. The self becomes identified with the whole range of things within which I have immersed myself. I am the person who does this, says that, behaves in this or that way: a person who has an identifiable character to the extent that I am consistent in my views, actions and inclinations. But that objective self is no more a physical entity than was the internal, perceiving "I". True, what is described is the activity of my physical body (including my language), but it is no more a physical description of the body itself than a description of a symphony is that of the instruments that are performing. It is not what the orchestra *is* that constitutes the symphony, but what it *does*. Now, this objective account of a person creates no fundamental problems. It reflects what we all do as we describe one another; it is the basis on which we make friendships.

The problem is knowing how to relate that objective self to the experience of being "me", for I experience myself in a way that is quite different from the way in which anyone else experiences me. And it is that personal sense of self that is, I believe, a necessary and useful illusion.

Of all the world philosophies, Buddhism takes the most radical approach to the self. It argues, as a fundamental and universal truth, that there are no fixed selves. This is the teaching known as *anattā*, and it applies to everything, not just to human beings. It reflects the Buddha's teaching that no compound thing is fixed or permanent. Buddha taught that what we regard as the self is actually a bundle of five *skandhas* (which may be literally translated as "heaps"), which are themselves in a constant state of change. These *skandhas* are our physical body, our sensations, our perceptions, our mental formations and impulses and our consciousness. Notice the sequence here. It describes a process in which the information that comes to us through the senses is interpreted to give us understanding of the external world and impulses to react to it, and from this springs consciousness. This is not a million miles from the process we described earlier as mapping: it is a gradual laying down of experiences, evaluating and responded to them, in a way that builds up our consciousness of self. In other words, in Buddhist philosophy, the self is a process, not an object. It is a process that gives consciousness to the physical body, but – like a camera that can photograph everything except itself – it cannot itself appear within the world that it maps out. I can experience being "me", but I cannot describe what it is to be me, for any description has to be made using the sort of categories that we would use of anything in my experienced world. But I am not *in* that world; I am here experiencing that world. Everything else I can describe is "out there", located in time and space. Even my own body is physically located, and I can mentally detach myself from it. I have no problem inspecting my toenails or locating a pain!

But my experience of being "me" is not physically located; it is a process.

Trying to be self-consciously aware of yourself at every moment is a brain-hurting exercise, and one that is largely unnecessary. It also gets in the way of pure experience. Reflexive self-awareness may indeed have been a great leap forward in evolution – we are aware that we are aware; we can ask questions about "me" – but at a practical level it causes problems. Two common examples will suffice. Watch someone new to ballroom dancing take to the floor and attempt a quickstep. You can almost feel their brain working overtime as they try to coordinate movement, music and a set of instructions. They are utterly self-conscious, desperate to get it right, and the result is wooden. Watch a new driver, out on the road with an instructor, fumbling for gears and getting into a panic at roundabouts. In both cases, their actions are dominated by the self-referential nature of their awareness. Not just "this is how I change gear" but "Oh, my God, there's a car coming and I have to get out of here!" The experienced dancer or driver just does it, enjoying the flow of events; the learner is mostly concentrating on his or her vulnerable self.

Taoist philosophy has given the world the concept of *wu wei*, usually translated as "non-action". Taoism is all about naturalness, going with the flow of the Tao. So it emphasizes that, for an action to be natural, it should not be forced or go against the natural grain of events. *Wu wei* does not refer to inaction, but to natural action: simple, effortless, achieving its goal with minimum destruction of the world around it, operating with a sharp instrument rather than a bludgeon. Transfer that to the idea of "no-self" (which is a reasonable way of expressing the Buddhist *anattā*). No-self is what happens when, in pure awareness, life flows in unselfconscious naturalness. In the best of moments – of creativity, or ecstasy, or joy – there is a complete loss of self. When the "I" is totally engaged, the "me" disappears. Think of a moment when you were engrossed in something. Did you exist in that moment? Clearly, the conventional answer is that, yes, you did, but that is because we have to assume the continuation of a self between specific moments of self-awareness. But when engrossed, you are acting in a way that is totally other-regarding. You are, literally, "lost" in what you are doing.

All genuine creativity is a loss of self-awareness. At the moment of intensity, when the conductor, by his look and the movement of his baton, drags out the last drop of emotional intensity from a Rachmaninoff symphony, or when the painter is engrossed in the application of a particular, subtle colour, the conscious mind is stilled, self-awareness vanishes and the mind is fully engaged. Indeed, a performance "takes off" once self-awareness is shed, and the performer is at one with the work being performed. There is plenty of self-conscious art, but it is mere imitation. It uses the same tools or media as true creativity, but puts them to the more mundane task of expressing an individual, social or political idea. That is presentation: it may be beautiful but is likely to remain derivative. Creativity pure and simple goes beyond that; it involves plunging the self into the deep waters of reality, oblivious of "me".

Many years ago, shortly after reading Robert Pirsig's *Zen and the Art of Motorcycle Maintenance*, I went out and bought a motorbike (well, to be honest, a Honda 50 moped). I craved the sense of the open road, the experience of being alive, free and hurtling through a landscape, aware of the shifting patterns of warmth and the changing surface of the road. I wanted deliberately self-conscious experience; I didn't just want to be there, I wanted to feel that I was there. But later, having become used to chugging through London at a maximum of thirty miles per hour, the Zen sense of wonder evaporated, and the daily commute became routine. I ceased to think about the experience *as* experience. I no longer thought that it said anything about me: it was just the way I travelled. The self was removed from the experience.

There is another sense in which the self can vanish. In Iris Murdoch's novel *The Bell*, and elsewhere, we find the idea that the "good life" is one that is lived out without any preconceived image of oneself, and that preoccupation with oneself and one's image is a narrowing of one's humanity. Contrast this with its opposite, displayed in the character of Jane Austen's Mr Collins. Hypocrisy is but an inflated, sham version of all attempts to behave in ways that consciously reflect what we wish to believe ourselves to be, whereas it's when you forget yourself that you are most fully real and alive. This distinction between the moments of self-forgetful immediacy and spontaneity and those of self-conscious calculation is crucial for the way we engage with the world and with other people. We have already noted that, in Buddhism, the enemy to happiness is the natural tendency of the unenlightened to grab and grasp at that which is pleasant, and to run from that which is unpleasant. And this is the result of our self-conscious sense of "me".

Sartre loathed stickiness. When you touch something sticky it clings to you and, if you want to be free, you need to shake it off. When you seek out and touch things you want to be free in your exploration of the world, but once you find yourself entangled in sticky things your self suddenly starts to lose its freedom: it becomes trapped, it fights its way out of a clinging jungle craving freedom of movement. Sartre's fear is to have his freedom curtailed in this way. People, careers, our own past, our self-images: all these things and more can become sticky for us – can cling on to us and define us, can prevent our free movements. Contrast this view with the one we have been exploring above. If we are obsessed with the freedom to be "me", we will always feel threatened by the sticky things of this world. When we engage spontaneously, with no conscious sense of "me", we become Teflon-coated; there is nothing to which the sticky things of life can cling. Spontaneity implies freedom. To be unself-consciously engaged is to see things for what they are, not for what they may do to "me". Those who try to maintain their own position have to be careful that they mix with the right people, for undesirables would become sticky and polluting: people who would need to be shaken off. Those who act without sense of self see all people as interesting, rather than threatening. And the tradition of this is seen in such figures as Jesus or the Buddha, who seem to have been willing to engage with all kinds of people without prejudice.

In yet another approach to this same phenomenon, Mark Vernon (in his book *Wellbeing* in this series) argues that, in spite of the tendency of post-Enlightenment humanism to focus on this-worldly satisfaction rather than a striving for some heavenly goal, and the sense that the only values are those that we generate, there is a place for transcendence. This is the recognition that the individual is not the centre of things, but can find value, meaning and wellbeing in that which is beyond the self. It may be experienced in friendships and in commitment to a cause, and in both cases the sense of "me" is enlarged to take into itself the friend or the cause. And this highlights a long tradition within Western philosophy and religion, where happiness – or the more broadly based idea of wellbeing – is achieved through a process of going beyond the limited range of understanding and concerns that focus on the individual.

In all these ways, self-consciousness gives way to a natural sense of something beyond, something higher: the natural flow of a dance that the beginner cannot experience while looking at his or her feet, or thinking one step at a time. But, in terms of the way in which our minds work, transcendent selflessness, however natural it may be to those who experience it, does not come easily, and certainly not through introspective analysis. Hume pointed out that, whenever he contemplated his own mind, he found in it a procession of things and events. The mind is always self-cluttering. This is clear to anyone who has attempted meditation. The task is to clear your mind, to become solely focused on the object of meditation, but it is *so* difficult. After a few seconds of calm inactivity, the mind barges in with all manner of irrelevant thoughts, challenging why you are bothering to meditate at all, or commenting on the surroundings, on what you will do tomorrow, on almost anything. Thought, like nature, abhors a vacuum. Setting aside the stream of mental chatter takes a good deal of practice. Being calmly aware without becoming dominated by mental clutter sounds easy, but it is extremely difficult to sustain for more than a few minutes. But, once sustained, it is used in a Buddhist context to reinforce the sense of no-self, and to release the meditator from the self-destructive tendency to grasp and crave and make everything self-referential.

The illusion of "me" also has implications for the experience of freedom. On the one hand, science will always strive to explain everything. Whatever I do, it can be exhaustively explained in terms of the flexing of muscles, the firing of neurons and so on. Yet, at the same time, I experience myself as free. That freedom is, in physical terms, a necessary illusion. You make a decision, you freely choose to do something: that is real, and you are a real part of the physical universe. Yet, as soon as you stand back and attempt to analyse it, freedom vanishes; it is colonized by the empire of explanations. And all too often we collude with explanations and avoid thinking about the freedom of the self. Sartre saw that, through fear of freedom, people tended to allow themselves to take on a fixed role in life – to act in "bad faith" – rather than have to live with the dilemmas of what one should do. We saw the same thing in terms of Heidegger's idea of the conventional masks that people wear. Existentialism focuses on the "I" that chooses what to do, that sets goals. That is the starting-point of philosophy, not a conclusion to the question about whether freedom or the self is possible. We know it is possible because we experience it.

The self that stops and asks about whether or not it is free is already unfree. That is simply because it assumes the reality of an entity called "me" over and above the actions that I carry out as an experiencing subject. But – and this is clear from Kant – we cannot perceive things as they are in themselves, but only as we experience them to be. When I look at myself as though a separate object (called "me") I am looking as though at another person: I am making myself an object to be observed. And, of course, once I do that, my freedom to act vanishes, because – by definition – everything that I experience has a sufficient cause (that's the way our minds work). If the experienced world had genuine freedom, predication would be impossible. We have to assume that we can always (given enough background information) explain the actions of others, while at the same time knowing that we ourselves can act freely.

At the end of the *Tractatus*, Wittgenstein pointed out that whatever can be known can be put into words, but that a sense of the world as a whole cannot be included in the list of things that are known through the senses, and therefore cannot be described. He ended that book with the now famous claim: "Whereof we cannot speak thereof we must remain silent" ([1921] 2001: 7). That reflects Wittgenstein's interest in mysticism. There are things of which the subject self is aware but which are beyond the world of empirical evidence and certified claims to knowledge. And it is this transcendence of the mundane catalogue of objects that suggests the problems we have with "me". The eye that sees cannot see itself directly; the self that experiences cannot experience itself. Faced with that dilemma, this elusive, indefinable "I" casts around for a way of describing itself to itself, and comes up with "me". But that is an illusion, albeit a necessary one. Kant made the distinction between the unknowable things as they are in themselves and things as we perceive them to be. Similarly, in ninth-century India, Sankara argued for a distinction between Nirguna Brahman (unqualified reality) and Saguna Brahman (qualified reality), the former known only through pure consciousness, the latter seen as acting, perceived in images. Similarly, Mahayana Buddhism sees two different levels of reality, the absolute and the conventional.

We cannot function if our only perceptions are at the absolute level of reality. In practice, we need concepts and images that enable us to get a handle on life, to deal with it pragmatically. Those on a quest to find some absolute location for "me" amid their neural synapses are going to be disappointed. At the absolute level, and the level in which we dig down into physical reality to the point at which we are looking at pure energy, or at the operation of sub-atomic particles, the "me" will have no place. "Me" is a necessary illusion, a fiction that enables us to deal with the world in a way that is meaningful. It is the central focus of the map of significance that we construct and superimpose on the world of sense experience. It is the point of convergence of all the lines that connect this perceiving subject with the things that it values. So what is it like to feel the self as an illusion, or, more accurately, as a process rather than an entity?

At this moment, as I look straight ahead of me, I see the walls of my study, books, files, dead spiders (yes, I am reminded of the need to dust), photographs of those dear to me. And as I sit I am aware also of the value that I place on these things, and the significance of this room for me, and my mind starts tracing its map, following my eyes to name and give value to everything I see. And I am conscious of inhabiting the space between my ears. In fact, I can feel my glasses, hooked on my ears, but see them only as increasingly out of focus as they go out of my field of vision. And most of the time I am thinking (and typing) and self-aware. And that awareness is the voice running in my head. And I assume that is "me". But now I try consciously to still the process of sensual hunting. I try to see without looking; to be aware without thinking; to feel that there is a process going on without thinking of an entity ("me") trying to direct it. It is difficult to remain aware and yet disengaged. The self tries to get back into the picture; the voice in the head demands to be able to comment, if only on the foolishness of trying to eliminate it.

The sense of a personal "me", physically existing in this world alongside our senses, our brain and the rest of our body, is indeed an illusion. "Me" refers to the continuous process by which the elusive "I" (the experiencing subject) finds its way around the world and builds up a personal map of meaning. It is not *part of* the physical world (and will never be "explained" in terms of neuroscience), nor is it part of a separate mental world. Rather, it is the experience generated by a process that starts from the moment a baby opens her eyes and starts to root around for what she needs.

Postscript: where does that leave "me"?

This book started with the idea that when we take a photograph, or encounter someone, we sense that there is a real "person" or "character" whom we can know and to whom we can relate, and therefore that, when others see us, they encounter someone whom I refer to as "me". But the question has been: what is that "me" and how does it relate to my experience of being myself? Various options have been considered and eliminated. "Me" cannot simply refer to the neural activity that goes on in my brain. It is intimately related to it, of course, and if there were no brain activity I would not be here as a functioning, sensing, thinking being. Indeed, I could not live without the operation of the brain in controlling my temperature and other systems. My brain is crucial to my existence; it makes possible the complex processes or experience and response and all the elements of memory and intentionality that I experience as being "me", but that's not the same thing as saying that the brain *is* me.

But it is equally difficult to think of people as mental entities radically different from their bodies, for all that we know of other people is mediated to us via their physical gestures: what they say and what they do. That's not to deny the value of what psychology reveals, or the deeply ingrained sense that we are more than our physical bodies, but the idea of a disembodied self does not match our everyday experience, where people are fully embodied. We cannot escape from that base in neural activity, and nowhere is that clearer than in the sad case of degenerative brain disease, in which the person diminishes, their character erodes and they lose not only their intellectual capabilities but even their ability to recognize those closest to them.

As I sit here typing, I know that my brain is at work and that my various bodily systems are functioning in a controlled way to keep me alive. There is a closed physical system that involves this computer screen, light waves, the retinas of my eyes, the neural activity in my brain, the twitching of my fingers on the keyboard and the resulting change to what I see on screen. There is no gap in that causal chain into which I can insert "me". Nor should there be, for I am not a minor component in this process of typing, but the agent of the whole thing. What is difficult to explain is exactly how the experience of the mental life is related to that physical world. That problem has led to a vast literature exploring the problems of the philosophy of mind. That philosophical journey has some amazingly challenging and relevant moments, including the battle between materialist and dualist positions, and some wonderful thought experiments, such as John Searle's "Chinese Room" and Thomas Nagel's "What is it like to be a bat?". There is no scope to review them here, but they are widely discussed in the literature, and raise fascinating mental conundrums. Yet I find few of the traditional questions relevant or their answers convincing. We all have the experience of being a self, and we know that we experience other people; that is the most fundamental conviction, and without it all that we know of social interaction would be impossible. Seeing how the self works and develops should be obvious, not a mystery.

The idea of what constitutes a person has profound moral and legal implications. How should we treat people? When does life begin or end? When does it have legal status? When is it worth preserving? Should we always treat people as ends rather than means? What of so-called "saviour siblings", born to give genetic material to a sick brother or sister? What of hybrid embryos? Or abortion? Or euthanasia for those in a persistent vegetative state? In discussing all these issues we may want to ask: does this person have a unique nature to be protected? The problem is knowing how you define that unique nature. And when it comes to the treatment of other species or the environment as a whole, there is the additional problem of considering to what extent other animals also have selves to be respected and protected. The awareness of who we are may help us to empathise with other selves, and indeed with all other living things. So what do we know about that embodied self, mind or person that I refer to as "me"?

The mind is active and engages with the world through the senses. Through the process of choosing goals, seeking to make sense of life and mapping out those things that are important to us, we develop a framework of meaning and value, a map scaled to fit exactly our experienced world. We have therefore argued that the "me" to which I refer when I speak of myself, and that other people are able to describe and relate to, is not a fixed *entity*, but a *process*: the process of personal experiencing and mapping. The self is an ever-changing and developing process, built up over time. It would be possible to speak of it in terms of a web, or a narrative (both images used by Dennett), but the image that I recommend in this book is that of an ever-developing, interactive map, an image chosen because it reflects the way in which the active mind plots out points of significance and locates itself at the centre of a world that is filled with meaning and significance.

If it were not for the ability of the brain to store and recall experiences we would have no more than a rudimentary personality, for we would have to start afresh to evaluate experience every time. As it is, we build up a database of previous experiences that gives us the ability to make choices, predict results and express preferences. And, as we do so, we build fresh overlays for our personal map, establish new journeys to travel and locate new points of value. The fact that the map is always being revised – growing with every new experience – ensures that the self is not a fixed entity. I am and will always be open to change, and the attempt to stop that happening is an attempt to focus only on elements laid down in the past. On the other hand, the self is not simply the changing, mapping process in itself, for that would not account for the continuity through life. The sequence of overlying maps gives the balance between change and continuity, which best accounts for the experience we have of people remaining the same – traits laid down in childhood remain – while physically, intellectually and socially they may go through dramatic transformations. But the map is most certainly not experienced as "in my head", but out there across my world, and that is what gives me this sense of looking out into the world. My eyes do not just receive and record light, they go looking; my nose does not just smell, it sniffs; even my ears prick up when they hear something of interest; I relish new tastes, and my fingers go touching and exploring surfaces. Link such active senses to a brain and you have a sensitive and interactive machine: the generator of what we call "me".

The "I" is the point from which I gain my perspective on the world, experienced (appropriately enough) as coming from between and behind the eyes. But that point of perspective creates the illusion of a "me" that exists separate from and alongside the body. Being aware of the illusory nature of the self does not adversely impact on ordinary life, because in ordinary life we live happily with all sorts of illusions. What is not in doubt is that the content of the "me" that I experience is gradually established by the brain in subtle ways, as different areas assess and lock together the varied elements of my experience. This is not to make the self some kind of "epiphenomenon" – a by-product of neural processing – for that would suggest that the brain initiates the self. Rather, the sense organs and brain together form a sensing, evaluating and responding machine, out of which the self can grow.

It is the ability to remember that allows character to build. To describe "me" is to describe my map and the history of my mapping. Others see it only in terms of knowing what I have done and how I have responded to each situation (the art of the biographer); I know myself through memory of what I have done, experienced and felt. I know myself also through the inner mental dialogue, which evaluates and selects between experiences. This book has argued that "me" is the shorthand, conventional term we use for the set of directions, values and coordinates that define my ongoing experience. Of course, if we were free from our past and the characteristics it has given us, we might be absolutely creative with every moment, free to see exactly what is there, uncluttered by the preferences and prejudices that litter our personal space. But that would require the "me" to vanish from our everyday living.

Selfless action is admired universally, and promoted by all the great religions. To set self aside and go for something higher, to give one's life for a cause, to be absorbed in a sphere of work, or a society, or a family, is a great thing. The self is enhanced to the extent that it is not self-referential: to the extent that it looks out and finds its joy and its future in that which is beyond itself. But for most of us, most of the time, life is rather more mundane, and we find ourselves contemplating what we should do, and reflecting on this necessary illusion called "me".

In one sense, of course, the self is certainly not an illusion: it is the path we trace out through life; it is what we are to others; it is what we put down on our curricula vitae; it is the self that is involved, public, known; that has been born into a particular time and place; thrown into the circumstances that appear to define it. But what we have been exploring here is the way in which our sense of "me" is built up, and how it is maintained. And that is where the interactive process of mapping comes in. It is curious to think that as crucial a phenomenon as the self is produced as a feedback loop, but that's effectively what it is. Let's explore the experience of being aware of that process.

I enjoy using Google Earth, seeing on my screen an image of the world unfolding beneath me as I appear to fly over continents. And, by opting to see various features, I can see roads and cities pop up on the terrain ahead as I approach them, bursting into view like targets in some shoot-'em-up computer game. I want to suggest that a similar thing is happening in our everyday, waking life. I look around as I walk and see things of interest; and as I do so, there is a monologue running in my head, commenting either on what I see, sorting ideas and memories triggered by the experience, or perhaps on my emotional engagement – boredom, excitement and so on. But where is all that coming from? It is the feedback from the brain, sometimes in direct response to the present moment, sometimes from the more convoluted self-reference of intellectual enquiry. That process of stimulus and response, of habitual reactions and emotions, built up over years, brings with it a familiarity: we know what we think, we have our likes and dislikes, we know how we react emotionally. And that massive, cross-referring, subtle, neural database located in our heads gives us the impression of a subject self: indeed, when linked to our senses and interacting with them, it becomes the vehicle of our subject self.

The self is the most sophistical and brilliant illusion imaginable. From the basic need of sentient creatures to find food, mate and avoid becoming food has developed this mechanism for interpreting the significance of what the senses reveal. And each member of the species *Homo sapiens*, with 100 billion neurons available in its head, has the tool with which to develop this invaluable illusion: the "I" between the eyes looking out; the "me" that I believe myself to be. And the joy of it is that what may be an illusion when I consider myself from an objective point of view becomes a reality as I encounter it in other people. In every word and gesture, shared emotion and common enterprise, I gain genuine knowledge of the real "you". You are not some hidden, mental thing, always out of reach, but a growing, changing map of hopes and fears, values and qualities, which I can know as part of my world, and that you can share with me. I cannot know everything about you, for you can never share with me the whole of your interactive map, even if you wanted to, for much remains hidden in your unconscious. But the solipsism that lurks behind the old dualist view – the world of unknowable mental selves with bodies attached – or the denial of a real "you" that I can relate to, implied by a materialist reduction of all reality to the level of neurons, has gone.

There is no mystery to consciousness: no secret, hidden "me" waiting to be discovered; no ghost in the machine. A human person – described as "me", experienced as "I" – is simply the most wonderful product of an evolutionary process that allows senses and brain to work together. And the most amazing thing is that it not only gives character to characterless neurons and sense organs, but it also transforms the external world of physical matter into one that is mapped out with value, beauty, friendship, meaning and significance.

Further reading

Here are just a few books that I would like to recommend for those interested in following up on the issues. For those who want to know more about neuroscience, *Creating Mind* by John E. Dowling (New York: Norton, 1998) is a wonderful and very readable guide to the way the brain works, its basic architecture and how it relates to the rest of our body and our experiences, illustrated by case studies of the way in which physical problems with the brain impact on people's lives. It doesn't just tell you about neural activity, it shows what it means in practical terms.

The Kingdom of Infinite Space by Raymond Tallis (London: Atlantic, 2008) celebrates the amazing features of the human head as the point of reference for our experience of the world, teasing out the subtleties of communication and the wonders of the various biological systems that we tend to take for granted. Read this book and the life that goes on above your neck will never seem quite the same again.

Daniel Dennett's *Consciousness Explained* (Harmondsworth: Penguin, 1991) really needs to be the starting-point for the modern discussion. Although unfairly dismissive of Descartes's dualism, his materialist view of the self as the "narrative centre of gravity" is an intriguing way of reconciling the physical world with subjective experience. There is also his *Freedom Evolves* (London: Allen Lane, 2003), which explores the phenomenon of freedom and challenges traditional assumptions of determinism. Dennett can be crude in his dismissal of views with which he does not agree, but his lively and challenging style brings home the real issues, and his conclusions are not far removed from those of this book.

For a thorough and erudite survey of the philosophy of mind and the cognitive sciences, there is *Mind and Cognition: An Anthology*, edited by William G. Lycan (Oxford: Blackwell, 1999). This includes articles by many important thinkers in this area that this book has been unable to accommodate, including U. T. Place, Jerry Fodor, Hilary Putnam and Paul Churchland. This gives a solid grounding for further academic study.

But for a simpler introduction – if you will forgive a personal advertisement – there is my own *Teach Yourself: The Philosophy of Mind* (London: Teach Yourself Books, 2003), which gives a survey of the traditional debates, and introduces many themes relevant to "me".

References

Beauvoir, S. de 1948. *The Ethics of Ambiguity*, B. Frechtman (trans.). Secaucus, NJ: Citadel Press.

Beauvoir, S. de [1949] 1972. *The Second Sex*, H. M. Parshley (trans.). Harmondsworth: Penguin.

Buddha 1973. *Dhammapada*, J. Mascaro (trans.). Harmondsworth: Penguin.

Camus, A. 1948. *The Plague*, S. Gilbert (trans.). Harmondsworth: Penguin.

Dawkins, R. 1976. *The Selfish Gene*. Oxford: Oxford University Press.

Dennett, D. 1991. *Consciousness Explained*. Harmondsworth: Penguin.

Dennett, D. 2003. *Freedom Evolves*. London: Allen Lane.

Dennett, D. 2008. "Autobiography," in 3 parts. *Philosophy Now* **68–70**.

Descartes, R. [1637] 1960. *Discourse on Method*, A. Wollaston (trans.). Harmondsworth: Penguin.

Eliade, M. 1959. *The Sacred and the Profane*. New York: Harcourt Brace.

Freud, S. 1930. *Civilisation and its Discontents*. London: Hogarth Press and the Institute of Psychoanalysis.

Heidegger, M. [1927] 2008. *Being and Time*, J. Macquarrie & E. Robinson (trans.). New York: Harper & Row.

Hume, D. [1739–40] 1969. *A Treatise on Human Nature*. Harmondsworth: Penguin.

James, W. [1890] 1950. *The Principles of Psychology*. New York: Dover.

Jaynes, J. 1976. *The Origin of Consciousness in the Breakdown of the Bicameral Mind*. Harmondsworth: Penguin.

Kundera, M. 1984. *The Unbearable Lightness of Being*. London: Faber.

Locke, J. [1690] 2004. *An Essay Concerning Human Understanding*. Harmondsworth: Penguin.

Marcus Aurelius 1964. *Meditations*, M. Staniforth (trans.). Harmondsworth: Penguin.

Moore, G. E. 1903. *Principia Ethica*. Cambridge: Cambridge University Press.

Nietzsche, Friedrich [1883] 1961. *Thus Spake Zarathustra*, R. J. Hollingdale (trans.). Harmondsworth: Penguin.

Nietzsche, Friedrich [1882] 1991. *The Gay Science*, W. Kaufmann (trans.). London: Random House.

Plato 2007. *Republic*, H. D. P. Lee & D. Lee (trans.). Harmondsworth: Penguin.

Plato 1999. *Phaedo*, D. Gallop (trans.). Harmondsworth: Penguin.

Proust, M. 2003. *Á la recherche du temps perdu*, L. Davis (trans.). Harmondsworth: Penguin.

Rousseau, Jean-Jacques [1782] 2005. *The Confessions*, J. Cohen (trans.). Harmondsworth: Penguin.

Rowlands, M. 2008. *Fame*. Stocksfield: Acumen.

Ryle, G. 1949. *The Concept of Mind*. Harmondsworth: Penguin.

Searle, J. 2007. *Freedom and Neurobiology*. New York: Columbia University Press.

Tallis, R. 2008. *The Kingdom of Infinite Space*. London: Atlantic.

Vernon, M. 2008. *Wellbeing*. Stocksfield: Acumen.

Warnock, M. 1970. *Existentialism*. Oxford: Oxford University Press.

Wittgenstein, L. [1921] 2001. *Tractatus Logico Philosophicus*. London: Routledge.

Index